# SAFE AND SOUND

# A PARENT'S GUIDE TO DISCARDED CHILD PROTECTION

# Roderick Townley

SIMON AND SCHUSTER  •  NEW YORK

Copyright © 1985 by Roderick Townley
All rights reserved
including the right of reproduction
in whole or in part in any form
Published by Simon and Schuster
A Division of Simon & Schuster, Inc.
Simon & Schuster Building
Rockefeller Center
1230 Avenue of the Americas
New York, New York 10020
SIMON AND SCHUSTER and colophon
are registered trademarks of Simon & Schuster, Inc.
Manufactured in the United States of America

10   9   8   7   6   5   4   3   2   1

Library of Congress Cataloging in Publication Data

Townley, Rod.
  Safe and sound.

  Bibliography: p.
  Includes index.
  1. Child abuse—United States.  2. Child
molesting—United States.  3. Kidnapping—
United States.  4. Child abuse—United States—
Prevention.  I. Title.
HV741.T69   1985      649      85-11904
ISBN 0-617-54420-9

# Acknowledgments

The cooperation of many people was necessary for the writing of this book and I would like to thank the following: John Walsh, who suggested the book in the first place; Denny Abbott, Nancy MacBride, and Sharon McMorris of the Adam Walsh Child Resource Center, for helpful information as well as for permission to use portions of the *Safety With Strangers* manual; the National Center for Missing and Exploited Children for supplying me with the "model legislative packet" and many useful leads; FBI Special Agents Kenneth Lanning and Robert Ressler for explaining psychological profiling and other mysteries; former NYPD officer Anthony Mercaldi for background on the "chicken-hawk" syndrome in New York; Irving Prager and the University of La Verne College of Law's Children's Justice Center for permission to use material on child-safety legislation; Dr. and Mrs. Charles F. Rattray for welcoming me into their house and letting me reprint their letter to the Walshes; Richard Ruffino, executive secretary of the New Jersey Missing Persons Commission, for his unstinting help; my *TV Guide* colleagues, Robin Bilinkoff, Joanmarie Kalter, John Noonan, Jerry Vermilye, and John Weisman for providing a cheering section; my *TV Guide* editors for their forbearance; Sharon Rosenthal of *US* magazine; my agent, Lois de la Haba, and her associate, Luna Carne-Ross, for shrewd suggestions and unflagging faith; Susan E. Lee for her early encouragement of the project; and Wyatt Baker for her much-needed support and companionship.

A special thanks to my editor,
Patricia B. Soliman,
whose faith made this book possible.

*For my dear son*
*Jesse—*
*be safe.*

# Contents

# Foreword

This is a book all parents must read. It puts a weapon in their hands to help them protect their children. Until recently most of the psychological weaponry and the cleverest tactics seemed to be in the hands of those who prey upon our children. Even now these predators are counting on society's aversion to the problem of sexual abuse. They're counting on the natural human impulse to turn our heads away in disgust. Well, the stealing, maiming, molesting, and murdering of our children has got to stop. And I say we can no longer afford to turn our heads away in disgust. It is time for action.

Until our six-year-old son, Adam, was abducted and murdered, Revé and I would not have believed that such a thing could happen to our family. We were like millions of others who persist in believing that it is other people's families, not our own, who may be harmed. Since then we've learned that there is no single social or economic stratum from which child victims come. The exploitation of children knows no boundaries, and to assume that it couldn't happen to you is naive and dangerous. It happened not only to the poor black mothers of twenty-nine children in Atlanta, Georgia; not only to the five little boys of Mormon parents in Provo, Utah; not only to the thirty-three young victims of John Wayne Gacy in Chicago, Illinois; the stain of child molestation and murder reached even the United States Senate when the daughter of Senator Charles Percy was abducted from home and murdered.

In the past few years I've met hundreds of parents of missing or murdered children, and I've met hundreds of children who survived rape, molestation, abduction. These children have all said to me that they believed that Mommy, Daddy, Mr. Policeman, Mr. TV Super-Hero—somebody— would help them. But no one did. No one was there for them. Where are our children's defenders?

And when people ask me, as they do, to give the perspective of the victim, I have to remind them that I am not the victim. I'm the heartbroken father left behind. The real victims are the silent, helpless, trusting children. People must recognize that if they care about the quality of their children's lives, they're going to have to take active responsibility and not rely on the "Theys." If there's one thing I've learned in the last three and a half years, it's that "They"— the police, judges, legislators, child-protection agencies— cannot be relied on to protect our children. In our search for Adam, and later during our efforts to effect legislative change, Revé and I realized that we are the "They." The people reading this book, you and I, are the "They." We are the people who will change the system.

People often say to me, "What can I do? What impact can I have? How can one person help?" Number one, you need to talk to your children. You need to make them aware that they have the right to say no; that there are parts of their bodies that are sacred to themselves alone; that no one is allowed to touch them there without their permission; that if something does happen to them they should *tell*; and that you will do something about it.

But that's not enough. Somehow we have to provide for all those hundreds of thousands of children in the United

States who *don't* have good parents, or who have busy parents who will never tell them what they need to know. That's why we need to become involved in our school systems, making sure that psychologically approved safety programs are in the schools to teach children how to resist abductors and molesters and how to make themselves less of a target.

Beyond that it is crucially important to work for the passage of legislation, both on the state and national levels. Many people feel reluctant to get involved in "politics." But we've found it makes a tremendous difference when people call or write their representatives urging passage of child-protection bills. Within the last year twenty bills were passed in Florida and some forty-five in other states— mostly through grass-roots efforts. But that's nothing compared to what needs to be done. This book addresses that issue and presents a "model legislative packet" comprising a configuration of badly needed laws. Concerned parents should work for the passage of similar laws in their own states.

The truth is, children have very few rights in this country. Children's legislation has traditionally fallen through the cracks, not because of opposition, but because of inattention. There is no organized lobby for children, no money, no vote, no constituency. You'll notice that when the time comes to close out the legislative session—whether it be in the U.S. Congress or in individual states—all the political action groups, the lobbyists, the people who have donated money to the reelection campaigns, always manage to get their bills attended to. We need that kind of organized effort on behalf of children.

We need people, in short, who are willing to get involved. We need people who are informed about their local day-care center as well as about the bills in the U.S. Senate. We need people to donate money to organizations that are legitimate and worthwhile in their advocacy of children's rights.

We need people at the barricades and on the front lines in this struggle against the legions of exploiters and parasites and predators.

Those who prey on innocent children are as cunning and as persistent as they are cowardly. That is why we need to enlist every concerned parent in this growing national movement to make our society a safe place for children to grow up in. I, too, get discouraged. I've almost given up a number of times. But then I remind myself, it takes an incredible coward to murder a six-year-old boy. It takes an incredible coward to rape a twelve-year-old girl. But I believe that we, too, would be cowards if we didn't do something about it.

—JOHN WALSH

# Introduction

Child-search expert Richard Ruffino, a gruff-talking, heart-of-gold ex-cop with the Bergen County, New Jersey, police, says he was thinking of writing a book like this about missing and exploited kids. "You know what I was going to call it? I was going to call it *Who Cares?*"

Parents, of course, have always cared, always worried; but until recently many of us, myself included, assumed that our children would be fairly safe if we just urged them not to talk to strangers and to come right home after school. We were ignorant. We didn't realize how ineffectual such "wisdom" would be against the clean-cut, concerned-looking man who approaches a child in the school yard and says, "Your mother's just been hit by a car. Come with me!" We didn't understand the importance of working out (and rehearsing) a set of child-protection strategies of the sort outlined in Part Two of this book.

Matching the ignorance of parents was the stony indifference of our public servants. Ruffino and others had to pull teeth and kick behinds to get minimal cooperation for missing children cases. A twenty-four- to forty-eight-hour waiting period was routine before police would even take a report of a missing child. Judges were cavalier (sometimes they still are) in their handling of molestation cases. Missing children, sexually exploited children, physically abused children had a hard time finding a friend in court. Kids seemed to have no rights.

Then came a multiple-award-winning 1983 NBC TV movie called *Adam,* with strong acting by Daniel Travanti and JoBeth Williams. The story of John and Revé Walsh's search for their missing six-year-old son, Adam, and their subsequent struggle against bureaucratic indifference to change the ways such cases are handled, touched millions of people. It didn't *cause* the public to care about missing kids (public concern had been building at least since the Etan Patz case in 1978), but it proved a catalyst and rallying point for what has now become a national movement. Perhaps we weren't ready for it before. In the late 1960s, Vietnam and the civil rights movement occupied our attention; in the 1970s, we had Watergate and the women's rights movement. Finally, in the 1980s, with all that groundwork behind us, we're able to support the long-overdue *children's* rights movement.

Public awareness of children's issues has suddenly escalated beyond anything Ruffino would have dreamed. Well-written child-molestation storylines are appearing in TV shows like "Cagney and Lacey" and "Webster." In mid-1984, NBC ran a hard-hitting report called *Silent Shame: The Sexual Abuse of Children;* and a few weeks later PBS ran an admirable five-part series, "Child Sexual Abuse: What Your Children Should Know." In the fall of 1984, "Good Morning America" inaugurated a weekly feature in which photos of missing kids (excluding children abducted by parents) were shown on the air. ABC's TV movie *Something About Amelia* sensitively explored the subject of incest. A syndicated Missing Children Network televises three minute-long reports per week on over sixty TV stations around the country. In many areas pictures of missing children can be seen on milk cartons and supermarket shopping bags.

There's even a magazine called *Missing*. The subjects of child abuse and abduction have become journalistically chic.

It's gratifying that the press has taken up this long-neglected issue, of course. In fact, without the insistent and sometimes vociferous coverage in newspapers and on television, it's unlikely that the Missing Children Act of 1982 and many laws since then would have been passed. And it is a good thing that parents everywhere are becoming more alert to dangers.

What may be dangerous (apart from the morbidity of some of the coverage) is the edge of hysteria that sometimes tinges discussions of child safety. Suddenly, molesters, child murderers, child snatchers are lurking in every drugstore and gymnasium in the land.

"A psychologist in California tells me he no longer touches children in play therapy sessions," says Dr. Stan J. Katz, a psychologist who evaluates child-abuse cases for the Los Angeles Superior Court. "People are very fearful. I know of one preschool in New Jersey that's losing staff. The people who work there say, 'Not only are we underpaid; now we're being accused of molesting kids!' "

On August 3, 1984, two days after my conversation with Katz, the New York *Daily News* ran a screaming headline:

BARE SEX ABUSE
OF DAY CARE KIDS

and the subhead: "Nab 3 in Attacks on Tots, 4 to 8."

Thus broke the horror story of the Puerto Rican Association for Community Affairs (PRACA) day-care center in New York City. The scandal quickly led to the resignations of the commissioner of New York's $4 billion Human Resources Commission and one of his top deputies. It appears that as many as thirty kids may have been molested, and some of them raped. Hundreds of furious parents showed up at the center, screaming in outrage and shattering windows with baseball bats. Soon there were reports of sexual abuse at other New York day-care centers, and more arrests were made. All this was bewildering and frightening, especially since it wasn't clear what "molesting" really meant. Then came a brief report that focused the horror with glittering clarity: one little girl was diagnosed as having gonorrhea of the throat.

"I would kill," said a friend, with quiet intensity in his voice. A thoughtful, peaceable man with two beautiful (and unharmed) daughters, ages fourteen and twelve, he wanted to know what I thought about the idea of buying a gun, just to have in the house.

It was becoming difficult being a day-care worker in New York City. When one group of kids from the Triangle Day Care Center in East Harlem was being shepherded to Central Park, passers-by reportedly shouted insults at the teachers. An employee at another New York center said that after ten years of working there he suddenly didn't know how to respond to the affectionate hugs of the kids when they traipsed in each morning. What if someone misinterpreted his actions?

Inevitably, some divorce lawyers have begun exploiting what Dr. Katz calls the climate of hysteria. Katz cites the case of a woman filing suit against her former husband, saying he'd molested their two-and-a-half-year-old daughter in the bathtub. He'd apparently taken a bath with the tot and she'd poked at his penis (curious object that it is) a couple of times. He contends he told her to stop and she did and that was the end of it. The ex-wife argues that he shouldn't be allowed to have custody.

It's hard to know, from these sketchy facts, whether sexual abuse of the child or legal abuse of the father is taking place. What is clear is that a whole new legal area is opening up for lawyerly exploitation. Alleging abuse, says Dr. Ralph Underwager, a Minneapolis psychologist, "is a way to instant custody." And usually it doesn't require a criminal trial and conviction. A simple allegation in family court can result in instant removal of children and loss of custody. No wonder there are groups like the Minneapolis-based VOCAL (Victims of Child Abuse Laws) being set up to help people unjustly accused of molesting kids.

Of course the U.S. judicial system has a long history of frame-ups and foul-ups. Among the most egregious was the case of Hayden Jones, an aspiring test pilot who, in 1949 (at age twenty-five), was convicted on eleven charges, including sodomy. Five boys from a blue-collar section of Pittsburgh testified against him. Their ages ranged from eleven to fourteen. The defense was lackadaisical, the prosecution unusually aggressive, and it took the jury a scant thirty minutes to return a guilty verdict. His sentence: fifteen to thirty years in prison.

Seven years later three of Jones's alleged victims recanted their testimony, contending that a police inspector, looking for a quick conviction, had forced them to testify as they did. The judge receiving these new affidavits decided she didn't believe them. Jones remained in jail. After serving nineteen years he managed to convince another judge to review the case. It became evident that the original trial had been riddled with irregularities almost to the point of travesty. Jones was acquitted of all charges. But by then he was broken in body and spirit, suffered from emphysema and heart trouble, his life ruined. He found a job as a night watchman in a used-car lot and slept in the back room.

If you think that couldn't happen now, talk to Charles Daniels, convicted in 1979 of sexually attacking and attempting to murder a two-year-old child. In early 1985 the city of New York acknowledged that he'd been wrongfully convicted and imprisoned and agreed to pay him $600,000 in compensation. Meanwhile, Daniels had been beaten, burned, and scorned by the other prison inmates. "In prison they consider you a punk, the lowest kind of animal, if you did something to a child," he later told a reporter.

Such cautionary tales are worth keeping in mind as we explore the question of punishment, evidentiary reliability of child witnesses, and the state of the law (Chapters 17 and 19). The most usual case, though, is the *reverse* of Hayden Jones's and Charles Daniels's. Child molesters tend to escape jail terms if found guilty. Most often, they escape even prosecution. Children testifying against adults are often suspected of fantasizing or downright lying—though in fact they very seldom do.

In writing this book I've attempted to lay out everything you need to know to protect your child. At the same time, I've tried to avoid clanging unnecessary alarm bells that could arouse panicky feelings. Panic is exactly the *wrong* emotion with which to approach the problem of protecting children. Not only does it undercut the safety messages you're trying to impart, it can also lead to hasty accusations and injustices of the sort I've just mentioned.

Two general principles underlie the chapters that follow, and it might be well to mention them at once, so that you can keep them in mind as you proceed.

First, the most important way to protect your child is to maintain an open and loving communication with him or her. Most missing children, after all, are runaways. Almost by definition that means kids who have given up trying to talk with their parents. A lack of loving communication can also lead to lonely children within the home, children so hungry for affection and understanding that they may fall prey to the lures of child molesters. Asked what ordinary people could do to help keep children safe, Father Bruce Ritter of New York City's Covenant House (a shelter for runaways) said succinctly, "Let your children know you cherish them."

Criminologist Dr. Georgette Bennett agrees: "Fundamentally, it comes down to the relationship that you have with your children and the way that you communicate with them, and also the amount of love and attention that they get in the home. To the extent that their needs for love are fulfilled, they're going to be less susceptible to pedophiles [those who look to children for sex]."

Another thing about communication is that it's a two-way street. It's not simply a matter of telling a child what's good for him. Such an approach is usually ineffective, since kids don't listen to lectures; but it's also dangerous, since it implies that children should do what adults tell them to. No longer is it safe to equate the "good" child with the obedient child. To do so is to raise potential victims. Children must be allowed to lie at times, to say no, and to run from adults if necessary. The issue of child protection forces us to reexamine the nuclear family and the assumptions on which it is based. This is all to the good.

The second general principle to keep in mind is that in order to protect your children you have to "empower" them —give them, in short, the tools they need to protect themselves. The point of this book is not to create frightened children, but the opposite. Fear is an invitation. One of the greatest things we can do for our kids is to help them develop what might be termed "enlightened fearlessness." Teach them to be at all times aware of what's going on around them; have them take precautions; have them, if they want, take karate; but, above all, teach them to carry themselves with an alert confidence. The importance of attitude—fortified by information—cannot be overestimated.

They'll need all their wits about them, from what one hears. While writing two recent *TV Guide* articles about the TV movie *Adam,* I ran into some frightening numbers: some 5,000 kids reported missing every day, between 1.5 and 1.8 million per year. A word, though, about statistics. Many numbers relating to molestation and parental abductions come from private organizations whose samples aren't always scientific. The government's Unified Crime Report tracks most crimes, but molestation figures have to be extrapolated from the number of assaults involving family members, and the results aren't definitive. The National Crime Survey would give a more accurate idea, but it doesn't cover people under twelve years old. Even if it did, there'd be the problem of underreporting: most incest, molestation, or abductions by a parent are never reported. We don't know if there are a million or two million runaways. We don't know if there are 150,000 or 550,000 child-snatchings by noncustodial parents.

Even given the fuzziness of the statistics, I was stunned by the dimensions of the problem of child safety. But I also learned that by raising public awareness one can save many children. At the end of both *TV Guide* articles, photos of missing kids were printed. One young girl, missing for two years, saw her picture there and managed to find her way home. NBC also ran photos at the end of each showing of *Adam,* and eventually some forty missing children were found. Laws on the federal, state, and local levels have been passed in impressive numbers since 1982. "Safety With Strangers" programs and child-fingerprinting drives have caught on in many school districts. The FBI has changed its policies and will now enter missing-children cases more readily than it used to. Until 1983, there had to be a ransom note or evidence that state lines had been crossed before the FBI would step in.

Communities are banding together in child-protection efforts. Among other things, they're forming judicial watch committees to draw attention to judges who are too lenient on molesters. They're lobbying for stronger laws to be passed. They're making sure that effective child-safety instruction is incorporated into school curricula. They're forming block associations that keep an eye out for the safety of neighborhood kids, designating certain "safe houses" where children can seek refuge if they feel threatened on the street. Parents should learn about (and help institute) such community efforts. As a start, they should become acquainted with local child-protection organizations, keeping relevant phone numbers handy at all times. Chapters 8 and 20 provide detailed information on these matters, and the Appendix lists many useful organizations to contact. Such groups should be contacted *before* anything bad happens to one's child.

A national movement is, in fact, in the making. And although child-sellers, pornography rings, serial murderers, pedophiles, and other predators still roam our society like sharks roam the sea, the word is getting out about them and nets are being dropped into the water. Among the most promising efforts is the Violent Criminal Apprehension Program (VI-CAP), run by the FBI in Quantico, Virginia. Launched in late 1985, the new program will weave a nationwide computer network to profile and snare mobile murderers who wander from state to state, killing as they go. Without such a centralized system, it's very difficult to catch these footloose psychopaths.

Beyond all our efforts, of course, there are the unknowables of life. No guarantees of safety are given any of us. And even with increased public awareness, children continue to be at risk. You can still walk into any shopping mall and find young children wandering about unattended. Hundreds of thousands of "latchkey" kids take care of themselves for hours after school, until their parents come home from work. And we're talking, for the most part, about good and well-intentioned parents.

Somehow, we hope that our love for our children will magically halo them and keep them from danger; but few of us can be certain of our power to bless. We watch them, these children of light, going forth into the world every day and trusting so simply that they will not be harmed. They are the blessings we count on, even as they count on us. By protecting them—and by training them to protect themselves—we are ensuring our own psychic survival. For which of us would not come to grief if anything should happen to them? As John Walsh, father of murdered Adam

Walsh, remarked with a sigh one evening as we were driving past the glowing one-family houses in the south Florida town where he lived, "Children are the true joy of this world."

## PART ONE

# What You Must Know to Protect Your Child

# 1

## Kidnapped

ADAM

The big Sears sign looms on the right as we speed past the mall, but John Walsh does not look at it. "I can't stand to go by it. I went there so many times with Adam and Revé."

On July 27, 1981, Revé Walsh, a blond, attractively athletic young mother, nosed her charcoal-gray, customized Checker car into a parking space at the Hollywood shopping mall in southern Florida. She wanted to check on some lamps that she'd heard were on special sale. Her son, Adam, a shy but good-natured six-year-old, was with her. This was to be just a quick stop. They'd come from the nearby St. Marks Lutheran School, where Revé had registered Adam for second grade, and were on their way home.

Inside the store an Atari video-game display caught Adam's eye; some older kids were playing and he wanted to watch. His mom told him she'd be just a couple of aisles away in the lamp department. He nodded. "I know where you'll be, Mommy."

Revé was gone just a few minutes. The lamps weren't

what she wanted. When she returned to the video display, the older kids were gone, and so was Adam.

Every parent has known that first creeping fear when one's child is not where he's supposed to be. Quickly she searched the nearby aisles. At any moment she expected Adam to turn the corner of a display case and run laughing to her. But this didn't feel right. Adam was an obedient child and not the sort to run off. A bright, happy boy with a talent for drawing, a love of sports, and a predilection for unusual hats (he was wearing a white cap that day), Adam was the Walshes' only child.

By coincidence, Revé's mother-in-law, Adam's beloved "Gram," came into the store. She found Revé crying. "Do you have Adam with you?" Revé asked desperately.

The two women searched the store and eventually the entire mall, while the store manager paged Adam over the public-address system. Something was terribly wrong.

The Hollywood Police Department happens to be just across the highway from the shopping mall. Anyone abducting Adam would have to drive right past the precinct house. Very soon the police were on the scene, searching and questioning. It appeared that the four teens at the video display had gotten to arguing, and the guard told all the kids, including obedient little Adam, to go out of the store. It was from there that the child had disappeared.

Adam's dad, John Walsh, a promotion and marketing executive in hotel management, was called and he hurried over. A boundlessly energetic businessman with the bounce of a bantam boxing champ, the thirty-five-year-old Walsh was not of the temperament to stay at home and wait for word from the police. "I wanted to help any way I could," he recalls, "with my resources and my contacts, my airline buddies. We printed the posters ourselves and distributed them. Friends of ours lent us cars. Detectives worked forty hours without going home. It was incredible."

John and Revé Walsh practically moved into the Hollywood police station for the next week or so, fielding calls and plotting strategy with Lieutenant Richard Hynds, a twenty-five-year police veteran who was heading the investigation.

Hynds calls it "the most massive investigation I've ever been involved in." Having the Walshes staying at the police station was only one of the extraordinary things about the handling of this case, as the police pulled out all the stops they could think of.

Unfortunately, as Walsh realized after being there awhile, few people at precincts in other jurisdictions were reading the police teletype that was going out about Adam's abduction. "So I had my own office staff, eight people, stay up day and night, calling all the police chiefs and sheriffs in Florida. Over seventy percent of them didn't know Adam was missing. They'd never seen the wire!"

Looking back, Hynds agrees, "There is a problem in the system. We *are* hamstrung. . . . It's very frustrating."

Refrigerators on display at Sears were opened up to make sure Adam wasn't trapped inside one of them; but even that first day the search had spread far beyond the area of the mall. That night fifty Citizens' Crime Watch volunteers combed the entire city. By the next day hundreds of people were looking. The Walshes will not soon forget the three hundred truck drivers who took two days off from work to search for Adam. "They walked ten feet apart, searching a several-mile area. Burger King supplied the meals free of charge." There were also private planes, a Sheriff's Department helicopter, game wardens, and many other people joining the search.

A reward of $5,000 was quickly posted, and a number of donations swelled the amount to $120,000 in a week's time. Meanwhile, John and Revé Walsh were making frequent appeals for information on local news shows, joining search parties, trying desperately to get the word out about Adam. "I liquidated every asset I had and borrowed money and went broke looking for Adam," he recalls. "My partners fortunately paid a lot of my bills so I wouldn't lose everything."

Most frustrating of all for the Walshes during those grueling summer days of 1981 was the refusal of the FBI to officially enter the investigation. The FBI did provide some technical assistance with laboratory work, but they had a rule that there had to be a ransom note or some clear evidence of transportation across state lines before the agency could step in and bring its huge resources and sophisticated equipment to bear on the case.

Walsh kept urging the FBI to become more involved. The local people were marvelous, he argued, "but what if Adam is in Georgia? What if he was flown to Detroit? What if he's in a van heading to Alabama? You've got to open up your network."

One thing the FBI did have to offer was its National Crime Information Center (NCIC) computer, set up in the mid-1960s and used for the most part since then to trace stolen cars and boats. It's a huge data bank, which local police precincts around the country can access if they want to. But often they have too much pride in their ability to handle a situation themselves; also, they sometimes feel they've got enough local problems to worry about without tapping into information about crimes that occurred in other localities. At the time Adam was stolen, the NCIC was dependent on information supplied by local police departments, many of which simply did not use the system. Also at that time there were very few "descriptors" that the computer would take on missing persons. Now there are many more points of description that can be entered, but then there weren't. Among the few programmable bits of information were driver's license and social security numbers. "So it didn't work for children," says Walsh.

Anyway, he adds bitterly, "the FBI's priorities were on other things—white-collar crime, Qaddhafi hit squads,

Abscam sting operations." Searching for missing kids was a low priority for the FBI, he thinks, just as it was for many police departments, who tended to assume that a missing child was probably a runaway. There was no such assumption in Adam's case, of course, and because of the marketing skills of John Walsh and his business associates, a remarkable amount of publicity was generated. For two weeks Adam's picture was in the papers every day.

It was evident, though, that the only way the case would gain attention outside Florida was for the Walshes to have access to the national media. As it happened, Willard "Bill" Frederick, the mayor of Orlando, was a friend of one of Walsh's associates. Frederick, in turn, had been a college fraternity brother of David Hartman, host of ABC's morning show "Good Morning America."

He called Hartman, and Hartman responded by inviting the Walshes onto the show the following Tuesday, two weeks after Adam had disappeared. John and Revé Walsh eagerly flew up to New York and booked into a hotel room the night before their first appearance on national television. They were full of hope. At last they'd be able to get their message out to a wide public.

But at six-thirty the next morning the phone rang in their room. It was a representative from ABC. There was word that the head of a young boy had been found in a canal near Vero Beach, Florida, 123 miles north of the Hollywood shopping mall. It might be Adam's. Did the Walshes still want to go on TV?

While Revé slept John Walsh dialed his longtime family friend Jeff O'Regan in Florida and urged him to find out whatever he could about this and call him back.

In a little while, he did. He wanted to know if Adam had a filling on the lower left side of his mouth.

He heard Walsh asking his wife, and heard the answer, "Yes." He also heard her asking what Jeff wanted to know *that* for.

Walsh tried to minimize the horrible news. "I told Revé they'd found some remains but we weren't sure whose they were or the age." He didn't want her to be thrown into despair while there was still any cause for hope. They left for the studio.

Host David Hartman had also heard the news and asked them if they wanted to go on or not.

"I said, 'It's past that now. If it *is* Adam, if he's dead, then I've got to go on for all those other kids you're going to show." The plan was for Kristin Cole Brown, a spokesperson for Child Find, to appear with them and for photos of a number of missing kids to be flashed on the screen.

Hartman, reports Walsh, "was wonderful. After our little segment, he came up to me and said, 'You're a strong person and I respect you for coming here. Anything I can do to help you, I will.' And he hugged me. And when they called him to go back after the commercial he had tears in his eyes."

Walsh headed dazedly back to the hotel while Revé, her sister-in-law, Jane, and Kristin Cole Brown went out to do some shopping. Revé recalls feeling frozen with fear the whole time.

The phone rang in the hotel room. Walsh picked it up, fearing it was the Florida police or Jeff O'Regan. It was George Merlis, executive producer of "Good Morning America," and he sounded excited. " 'Look,' he told me, 'we're going to get you two on every show in New York. Stay in the city a few days. We'll get your son's name around.' "

Good news. Wonderful news. Yet all John Walsh could think was that it was too late.

Then the phone rang again. Walsh sank onto the bed clutching the receiver. The identification was now positive. It was Adam.

"We'd tried *so hard* and had so much hope," says Walsh, his voice still a little shaky three years later as he recalls that moment. "Everybody has such incredible hope that their child's alive when ninety-nine percent of them are dead!"

It was good, he thinks, that Revé wasn't there, because he tore that room apart. Chairs, bedsheets, tables—he ripped, shattered, or hurled whatever he could get his hands on. And when the hotel detective barged in to see what the rumpus was, he found Walsh lying on the floor gasping for breath.

Revé was sent for and told about Adam. "She was like a wounded animal," her husband recalls. "She was destroyed."

This is where the story usually ends in cases like this. Bottomless despair. The Walshes went into hiding for several weeks at a friend's house to escape the now-aroused and rapacious press. Their marriage suffered and seemed about to crumble, because all they could see when they looked at each other was unbearable pain.

"I thought I was going to die, after Adam," says Walsh. "I lost twenty-two pounds, and I only *weigh* a hundred and fifty. I was throwing up and crying all the time. I still miss him. I miss him so much. I miss his physical presence. Yes, I miss him mentally, but also we used to rough up, and I'd lie in bed with him and read him stories at night. I miss him terribly."

At one point he and Revé were thinking of moving to Ireland. "I hated this country, I hated the system that had let me down all along the way."

But when they finally returned to their house after weeks away, the Walshes were overwhelmed with the amount of mail that had piled up—some 22,000 letters, most of them offering support or asking for advice or begging for help. Walsh began feeling pressured to do something. People told him, "You have the platform, the forum, the contacts."

"And then I decided," says Walsh, his eyes flecked with tears, "that as much as I was feeling sorry for myself, it was Adam, it was Adam's remains that they found."

He began to appear on talk shows, discussing the plight of missing children and the crying need to reform the system. He learned that Senator Paula Hawkins (R-Fla.) had introduced a child-protection bill in the Senate some five months before Adam was murdered, and that Representative Paul Simon (D-Ill.) had introduced such a bill in the House several months before that. Both bills were in serious trouble.

Walsh agreed to appear again on "Good Morning America," this time with Senator Hawkins. Not long afterward, Walsh was on the "Donahue" show. The public reaction was immediate and emotional, and congressmen began looking at the pending legislation with a bit more attention. Moving Congress to action, however, is a little like getting a woolly mammoth to skip rope. "I'd fly hours to meet with some congressmen and they'd say, 'Well, I really don't have time for this issue now. I know you're on a crusade, but everybody's on a crusade.' Or, 'Don't you think you're overreacting?' My son was murdered. There's no such *thing* as overreacting."

Revé Walsh, meanwhile, was equally busy. Parents of missing kids from all over the country had been writing and calling for advice, and the Walshes decided to set up an information center. With John Walsh running around the country lobbying for support for the House and Senate bills, much of the work at the fledgling Adam Walsh Child Resource Center fell to Revé. Besides, says Walsh, "I told Revé, 'I can't talk to the mothers; I can't deal with it on a day-to-day basis.' . . . I don't know how she did it. She'd come home every night crying, destroyed. And we were trying to hang on to each other, crying, crying, with nothing in common anymore but the grief. But we clawed through it."

Often he'd sleep in his office, writing Senate testimony until four in the morning. "And that helped me deal with it. I didn't want to go home because I would go in Adam's room and lie on the floor and look at all his stuff. . . ."

So the Walshes threw themselves into the missing-children movement, determined that other kids should not die unnecessarily because of lack of coordination among law-enforcement agencies. Lieutenant Hynds of Hollywood, Florida, says he was "surprised we got as much coordination as we did" in the Adam Walsh case. Detectives from other jurisdictions offered to come in on their off-duty hours. Such gestures, says Walsh, "reaffirmed my belief in people." In the depths of his despair he'd begun to lose that belief: "I thought there were only two kinds of people, those who didn't care and those who murdered children. And now I found people who did care."

Paula Hawkins, for instance, became something of a hero for Walsh. "She's a grandmother and a Mormon and someone from the old school, and she may not be the greatest advocate of ERA, but I'll tell you something, she's a breath of fresh air up there [in Congress]. She's not a power broker, she doesn't belong to the club, and she focuses in on human issues. . . . She went and cornered the President and Ed Meese and James Baker on these issues—cutting through the red tape." Walsh found allies as well in Orin Hatch (R-Utah) and Arlen Spector (R-Pa.) and Strom Thurmond (D-S. Carolina). Walsh's villains were Pat Schroeder (D-Colo.) and Harold Washington (D-Ill.), both of whom walked out of a hearing where Walsh and other parents were testifying. And Representative Don Edwards (D-Cal.) was consistently obstructive to the legislation that Walsh and Hawkins were fighting for. Those three, says Walsh, almost succeeded in getting the bill killed. And the Justice Department was opposed to it as well.

The thrust of the Missing Children Act, as it came to be known, was to make the NCIC computer more useful in cases of missing children. The proposed legislation did not require that the FBI go out hunting for children, but merely that parents be given better access to NCIC. If their local police did not enter a missing child's name and statistics into the computer, the parents could go to the FBI and have it done by the Feds. The NCIC would be a huge clearing-house of information about missing persons and would maintain an up-to-date file on "unidentified dead."

All this sounds like simple, uncontroversial common sense, but the FBI was vehemently opposed to it. The higher-ups seemed afraid that there'd be a nationwide rush to enter information on every missing child, that federal agents would have to go chasing after runaways, that the system would be overloaded. They may also have had dif-ficulty swallowing the idea that parents would have some control over what information goes into that computer.

Walsh was irritated by some of the Justice Department's tactics. When an FBI man spoke to district attorneys in New Orleans, for instance, he reportedly said, "I hope you all realize that John Walsh is an extremely bereaved parent."

"Intimating," says Walsh, "that I was an irrational person on a Don Quixote quest."

And, most stunning of all, someone in the Justice Depart-ment was quoted as saying, "That couple in Florida can go pound salt!"

Walsh can smile about the remark now, because "it ac-tually helped the bill tremendously. It was a fatal blow to the Justice Department." The media had a field day with it.

Revé Walsh looks back with some bitterness: "All those buildings in Washington, all that classical architecture. It's just a facade."

Her outlook brightened a bit when FBI Director William Webster—perhaps under Administration pressure—asked the Justice Department to withdraw its opposition to the Senate version, and the bill passed. On October 12, 1982, President Reagan signed into law the Missing Children Act, declaring the event "a great day for Adam."

Well, all right. Actually, Adam wasn't having any great days then. All his days had ended fourteen months before. Sometimes rhetoric is hard to listen to. But the bill was good. And a few months later another document was issued that very few people in the media picked up on, but it was just as important. Mid-February, 1983: a memo "To all FBI field offices from the Director of the FBI."

Henceforth, it said, missing persons cases will be assigned a high priority. Also, henceforth, *no ransom demand* is required before the FBI can enter such cases. Furthermore, the crossing of state lines can be *presumed* after twenty-four hours. Also, keep parents informed about developments in their child's case, and help them enter information into the NCIC "where local police refuse to cooperate. . . ."

DAVID

The importance of this document cannot be overestimated. It may have affected the speed with which the FBI responded to an event that happened about two weeks later in the town of Vero Beach, Florida, just a few miles from where the decapitated head of Adam Walsh had been found.

A tow-headed little boy named David Rattray was playing in the yard. Inside the rambling, expensively furnished two-story house, the black maid was puttering about. A middle-aged white man, dressed in work clothes, came to the door. There'd been an electrical problem, he said, and he was sent to check on it. The man looked around outside for a while, poking around with the electrical panel, then he reappeared at the door. He needed to come in and check inside too.

The maid let him in, and after a couple of minutes of looking at the stove, the man suddenly pulled out a gun. "I want your TV," he said.

It's not quite clear what happened at that point. Apparently, as the terrified woman was being tied up, she thought of four-year-old David playing outside. Without her supervision, he might run out into traffic. Whether the idea of bringing him in was originally hers or the intruder's, the boy was called, and when he came in he was tied and gagged.

The Rattray home was wired with a sophisticated alarm system connected with the sheriff's office. But when the man went outside again to check that nobody was around, the panic-stricken maid was apparently too flustered to think of the portable alarm button. "She's really supposed to keep that handy all the time," says David's father, Dr. Charles "Chuck" Rattray, a prosperous general practitioner who has lived in Vero Beach for the past twenty-nine years.

The opportunity to press that "panic button" was lost, and the man came back inside. He picked up little David and said that if the doctor wanted to see his boy alive again, he'd have to come up with $400,000.

With that he drove off in the maid's car. He pulled into a nearby shopping center, where his own car was parked. He dumped the terrified child in his trunk and roared off.

Chuck Rattray's wife, Pam, was working in the doctor's office that afternoon. He recalls, "She knocked and got me out of the [examining] room and said—she was crying—and she said, 'Someone has David.' We usually had somebody pick him up from [pre-kindergarten]. I thought somebody had picked him up by mistake. . . . She said, 'No, someone's *taken* him, and they want money to get him back.'"

Dr. Rattray hurried out to the house with one of his grown sons from a previous marriage. A vigorous, hearty man in his mid-fifties, the white-haired physician had the temerity to start a brand-new family at a time when most men are disencumbering themselves from such responsibilities. Little David, his littlest, latest, last child, was clearly the apple of his eye.

Arriving at the house, he found the sheriff's deputy already there. A few minutes later the sheriff himself arrived and also an FBI man from nearby Fort Pierce. More FBI men began arriving, and during the next couple of days there were, by the doctor's approximate count, forty-two FBI agents in, on, or about the premises.

The maid tried to tell her story, and the people next door related that they'd seen a car leaving in a big hurry, with a blue van right behind it. So the assumption was made that the kidnapper had an accomplice. While waiting and hoping for the man to call with a ransom demand, the FBI men were immediately busy getting phone taps installed both at the home and on all four lines at the doctor's office. A special communications man named Rich Richardson was brought in from the Miami office, and another FBI specialist from Fort Lauderdale put in tracing instruments so sophisticated that they could give a caller's number instantly. The FBI also called the telephone company, asking them to put in extra lines immediately, so that if one phone was busy at the house another would be open at all times. Cooperation was quick.

The maid's car was located within forty-five minutes of the doctor's arrival home. Tracing equipment was installed a few hours later. FBI agents were stationed across the street, watching everybody who came past. They also had two planes equipped with infrared visual systems that allowed them to see at night. The FBI had clearance to halt all air traffic from the local airfield so that these two planes could take off and land at any time. An elaborate system of radio communication was put in place so that agents could communicate with one another no matter where they were.

Then they had to wait.

The rest of the day passed, and the night. No call. Several FBI men stayed with the family the whole time. The girlfriend of one and the wife of another brought over a change of clothes for them. Neighbors brought over food, including a big pot of paella. But nobody could eat, and nobody even tried to sleep.

The next day, Wednesday, was the doctor's regular day off and he was at home. The secretary at the office was taking messages as usual when the kidnapper called. "I'm sorry," he was told, "the doctor's not in today."

The man said he'd call again at the same time the next day, and he quickly hung up, afraid perhaps that if he stayed on the line the call could be traced.

The doctor was in despair. "I thought, 'Gee, that's really great! We've lost it now. This is it. We've blown it.' "

One of the FBI men tried to reassure him: "Look, you're going to get your boy back. The only thing this man wants is your money. It's in his interest to keep your son healthy and alive. All he can bargain with is a healthy child."

But the idea of waiting another twenty-four hours for a possible call was nerve-racking. And the weather was turning cold. Rain was in the wind as the temperature dropped into the forties. David had been wearing only a little T-shirt and a pair of pants. Was he indoors somewhere? Was he alive? How long could a slightly built four-year-old survive?

That brief first call, as it happened, had come in along with two other calls on other office lines. All three were instantly traced. The kidnapper had called from a pay phone near a convenience store in Wabasso, a town less than ten miles distant. Although the FBI had no way of knowing it at the time, the phone booth was just a couple of blocks away from where the man lived. He had a wife and grown children, it was later learned, and none of them knew what he was up to.

Chuck Rattray and his diminutive wife had to face a second night of desperate worry, while ten miles away their child's abductor no doubt tossed and turned in his own bed beside his unsuspecting wife.

Dawn came, and no call. Morning became afternoon. If the man meant what he'd said about calling back, now would be the time to do it. But there was no call. Chuck and Pam Rattray feared that they had indeed "blown it," that the kidnapper had killed the child and fled, deciding that the ransom idea was too risky after all. Their seven-year-old daughter, Laurie Ann, a lovely and sensible young girl, continued to have hope: "Oh, you don't have to worry about David," she said. "He's so smart he'll find a way to get out."

The cold, overcast afternoon edged toward evening and all seemed to be lost. Only later did they learn that the kidnapper had intended to call when he'd said he would, but his wife, who usually worked at a nearby Woolworth's during the daytime, had unexpectedly been told to come in late that day. So she'd been around the house while he paced, waiting for her to leave.

Meanwhile, Dr. Rattray was trying to get together $400,000 in cash. "Now let me tell you how accommodating people are when something like this happens," he says, still moved at the recollection. "Our banker stopped the deposit that they had going to the main bank in Jacksonville or Miami, and they took out $400,000 in cash, banded it all up, and made out a little note, which we signed. One of the FBI agents put his fingerprints on the top bill of each bundle, brought it all out here in a sack, and sat it on the pool table." There the Rattrays left it, hoping against hope that they'd have the chance to give it all away.

It was early evening when the call came. An FBI man picked it up, said he was the answering service and could he take a message.

The message was for the doctor to drive out to a nearby shopping center, by himself, and to look for a note by the second lamppost from the end.

Chuck Rattray admits to feeling just a bit rattled as the FBI folks strapped him into a bulletproof vest and wired him for sound. This was it.

He drove slowly toward the rendezvous in the empty shopping mall while an FBI man lay on the floor by the backseat. They were connected with each other and with the other FBI agents via radio hookup, and Rattray also had on recording equipment so there'd be a record of anything said.

"Anyway, we went over, and I had a *hell* of a time finding that note. Started at the wrong end." The lampposts were alongside a wall, and Rattray was sure the kidnapper was crouched on the other side of it, watching him from the underbrush.

"I went to every lamppost, just about, in that shopping center; and finally, the next to last one, I found it! I kept thinking he'd come out from the bushes. Nothing happened. I had been instructed by the FBI to stand there and read the note out loud, and that's what I did."

The note had a sort of map on it and some instructions, including the admonition "Don't bring anybody with you." As he read aloud, dozens of FBI agents began converging on the place he was told to drive to. It was a couple of miles away, beside a bridge adjacent to a golf course. Two planes were even now in the air, and with their infrared equipment they had already spotted the kidnapper waiting in the dark woods near the edge of the golf course. As the doctor arrived at the bridge, FBI men were taking their places all around the golf course and over at the nearby fire station.

He stopped the car. "Should I get out?"

The FBI man concealed in the backseat said, "No way. Stay here in the car."

"But I think I see another note over there by the drain. There's something white out there."

"Okay, go ahead, get it, but then get back in here."

Rattray clicked open the door and stepped cautiously out. The white "note" turned out to be an old milk carton.

"But as I was standing there, I heard somebody call out, 'Hello.'

"And I said, 'Yes! I'm here!' "

As the eerie conversation went on, Pam and everybody at the Rattray house was listening to it. So were the agents at the doctor's office. So were the men stationed around the golf course and the men circling overhead in the planes. Yet the two men seemed totally alone, locked in the intimate, urgent privacy of darkness. The kidnapper was perhaps thirty feet away, but invisible, in a stand of tangled trees.

"Is this where I'm supposed to be?" called out Rattray.

"And the voice, disguised as a woman's voice, said, 'Yes, you're in the right place. This is it.'

"I said, 'I want to see my son.'

"And he said, 'Your son is safe, everything's all right.' "

The doctor went back to the car and said to the FBI man, "Okay, he wants me to leave the money. What should I do?"

The agent told him to go out and talk some more, to make doubly sure he was the right person, and also to give the other agents a bit more time to get into their places.

Dr. Rattray said he would try. He opened the door and got out again. "Look," he said, "I've got to know a little bit more before I leave this money. I've got to know that you're the one. That you've got my son. Because a lot of people know what's been going on, and you could be anybody leaving this note." Rattray asked the figure in the woods what little David had been wearing. The man answered accurately, but then added that the information was in the newspaper, so anybody might know that.

The weird exchange went on another minute or so, but that's as long as the doctor dared to keep it going. He asked one final thing: "This money's real, and you can have it. Nobody's going to stop you from taking it. But I have to have some assurance that I'm going to get my son back unharmed."

The disguised, womanlike voice from the woods replied, "He'll be playing with his toys in your house tonight."

"Fine."

The doctor returned to the car. "What the heck am I going to do?" he whispered to the FBI man.

The agent hissed back, "We're trying to get word from headquarters. Just hold on."

But no word was coming through. At this crucial moment their end of the communication system went dead.

"Look," said the now-desperate doctor, "I can't blow this. I've got to do something."

"But we don't have the okay yet! What if they're not in position?"

"I know, but we can't get through!" the doctor said.

The agent took a breath and said, "Leave the money and let's get out of here."

Rattray grabbed the heavy bag of money and stepped out of the car.

"Where do you want me to put it?" he called out.

"Bring it this way."

The doctor lugged the sack in the direction the voice was coming from.

"That's far enough."

The moment had come. The doctor was leaving $400,000 in the middle of a field with no guarantee whatever that his son was safe.

"You know," he called out, "this is real money. I've done everything you've asked. Now I expect you to keep your word. I expect you to return our son."

He backed away from the money and returned to the car. Then, as the agents had instructed him, he drove away.

No one was going to stop the kidnapper. They were sure he had an accomplice who would kill David if anything went wrong. On the other hand, the man couldn't get away. The FBI planned to tail him, find the boy, and then pounce.

But again, not everything went as it was supposed to. The logical thing would be for the man to go out onto the road and be picked up by the accomplice in a car, then speed off. In fact, however, there was no accomplice. And the kidnapper, having at one time worked as a grounds keeper on the golf course, knew the area intimately. Instead of going to the road, he cut across the fairway. He'd parked his car a half mile or more away, on the other side of the golf course.

There were so many agents in place around that whole area that they couldn't all get out of the way. And the kidnapper, with gun in one hand and loot in the other, ran right into a startled FBI man just eight feet in front of him.

Suddenly he knew he was in a trap. He raised the gun to shoot his way out of it. But so many people were on that darkened golf course that a sheriff's man was able to run up behind the kidnapper and grab him. The man's arm jerked up, the gun went off, and he collapsed. He'd accidentally shot himself in the head.

It was a shot heard for miles around, thanks to the elaborate communications equipment installed by the FBI. Indeed, everyone could hear it except Dr. Rattray, whose set in the car was on the blink. Pamela Rattray, sitting on the stairs at home, miles away, heard the shot clearly and thought, "My God, he's shot David."

On the dark golf course, sheriff's men and FBI agents converged on the badly wounded man bleeding onto the green. The immediate thought was: "Now we won't be able to find David."

"Where's the boy?" one agent reportedly asked.

The man did not at first reply.

Another agent reportedly said, "Look, you're dying, tell us where the boy is."

Negotiations went on for a bit, apparently, but no one is saying exactly how they went or what pressure was applied.

Finally, though, just before lapsing into unconsciousness, the man apparently said, "He's in the trunk of the car."

"What kind of car?"

"It's white . . ." The man lost consciousness and immediately scores of agents and sheriff's men fanned out searching for a white car.

On a quiet little street called Cherry Lane, on the other side of the golf course, they came across a white Chevy. Two hefty FBI men, using a crowbar, ripped open the trunk.

Pamela Rattray, sitting at home, heard one of the men exclaim, "We've got the boy!"

Carefully, they lifted the child out of the trunk. He was bound hand and foot and his mouth was gagged. He was lifeless in their hands.

"He's not responding" was the next thing David's mother heard over the radio. And again she had to tell herself, "He's dead. David's dead."

About two minutes passed and she couldn't hear anything more. They were using artificial respiration on the child. It seemed, she now says, like at least ten minutes, not two.

And then an excited voice came over the radio: "He's opened his eyes!"

There was a lot of excitement and laughter and talking, much of which Pamela Rattray missed because she was so overwhelmed with the flood of released emotions. "David's alive!" she was telling herself, swinging from despair and horror to incredulous joy.

Chuck Rattray didn't hear a word of this. He and his FBI companion were driving with their dead radio to his office in town, where the kidnapper had said he would call in forty-five minutes to say where he'd left David.

"When we got to the office, we started to go in," recounts the doctor. "And suddenly everybody was pouring out of the office. There'd been five or six of them monitoring the phones. And they came out and they said, 'They got David! He's okay!' "

Dr. Rattray abruptly stops his narration. He surprises himself by bursting into tears. He's been voluble and excited talking about this until now; but suddenly, for several minutes, he simply cannot say another word.

Two years after those events, six-year-old David runs about the kitchen, full of excited life. He doesn't talk much about the experience he went through, but he does say he wasn't really unconscious when the FBI ripped open the back of the car. He would like to have it thought that he'd been playing possum, in case it was the bad man coming back to hurt him. He may have been playing possum, or perhaps, as his father is inclined to believe, he was in a "hypnotic state. That's the only thing that preserved him for that length of time."

For fifty-three hours, night and day, David had been kept bound and gagged in the trunk of the car. Occasionally, his kidnapper would open the trunk and give him a glass of milk, but then the boy would be shut in total darkness again. If he'd gradually withdrawn into a state like hibernation, it wouldn't have been surprising.

When he was fully roused and knew he was free, he asked the FBI men who were taking him home if he could have a hamburger. There was this brand-new McDonald's restaurant that he'd been wanting to try. They gladly stopped. In fact, the FBI folks, far from the dour types portrayed on "The Untouchables," were whooping and laughing. "Everybody was cheering and hugging, just really celebrating," says Pamela Rattray, smiling.

Early in the investigation, Mrs. Rattray had asked the FBI about the Adam Walsh case, which of course everybody in Vero Beach knew about, since Adam's remains had been found just a few miles away. "And the FBI men pointed out to us that since this thing with Adam Walsh, they were allowed to come in," says her husband. He continues, "It was all that publicity, I think, that awakened the FBI to the idea that, 'Look, we're the only ones that really have the resources to take care of this thing.' " Dr. Rattray says he's still amazed at how much manpower they could mobilize in a short period of time. "I can tell you this—had the FBI not been on this case, he'd have gotten away scot-free. We'd have never seen David. We'd never see the money. Nothing. I don't think there's any way [the local police] could have caught him."

Rattray is quick, though, to give the Vero Beach police their due. It was they who called in the FBI in the first place.

Putting aside traditional jurisdictional rivalry, they offered (and gave) the federal agents all the help they could. It was an exceptional case in that regard. The welfare of the child overrode all other considerations.

Some months later, after things had calmed down a bit, Mrs. Rattray sat down and in her small, careful hand wrote a letter:

> Dear Mr. and Mrs. Walsh:
>
> I know this letter is long overdue, but it is so hard to know what to say. My son, David Rattray, was kidnapped in March, but today he is home and safe. This is the only way I know to say "thank you." For it is because of your courage and efforts that the FBI was able to be in on the case within hours of the kidnapping. Thank you for help-ing to save our son. My thoughts are with you more than you will ever know. I hope and pray that you shall be filled with much happiness and peace.
>
> Again, thank you,
>
> > Most fondly and respectfully,
> > Pamela Rattray

## WHO ARE THE CHILD-STEALERS?

Fortunately, there are relatively few child-stealers, but they comprise a number of different human types. The man who stole David Rattray is getting to be something of a rarity. Most people tempted to kidnap a child for ransom are bright enough to realize that they probably won't get away with it. There are easier ways to make a dishonest living.

After it was all over, Dr. Rattray realized that he had met the kidnapper before. A dozen years earlier, the fellow had come into the doctor's office complaining of chest pains, and Rattray had done a series of tests. Finally, he concluded that the problem was heart trouble and he sent him to a hospital in Miami, where the man had bypass surgery.

Apparently something of a malcontent, the man blamed Rattray for his angina and had held a grudge against him ever since. For two and a half years preceding the abduction, he'd been mostly out of work. He'd never been very successful when he *was* working. One of his main jobs had been caretaking at the local golf course.

Financially pinched, he apparently thought again of the wealthy doctor, for whom he bore no great love. He began snooping about the doctor's neighborhood a week before the abduction. What his exact plans were may never be known, because he has been "incompetent" ever since shooting himself in the head out on the golf course. Incompetent, certainly, to stand trial. He may never recover sufficiently to talk about what he did.

Naturally, Pamela Rattray thought of the Adam Walsh case, both because the child's remains had been found nearby and because the FBI had behaved so differently in the Rattray case. But it should be mentioned that the two abductions have little in common. As criminologist Dr. Georgette Bennett notes, the kidnapping of David Rattray is "exactly the kind of case that the FBI would have acted on to begin with." John Walsh's strenuous efforts had no doubt sensitized the bureau to the urgency of abducted children cases, and FBI Director William Webster's memo urging immediate action provided further prompting, but the Feds are hardly ever reluctant to take on kidnap-for-ransom cases.

It's also worth noting that neither the Walsh nor the Rattray case involved a pedophile. There's a myth abroad in the land that pedophiles are behind the great majority of "stranger abductions" of children. They aren't. Sometimes women will steal young children as a replacement for the child they lost or could never have. Sometimes babies are snatched as a black-market commodity to be sold for illegal adoption purposes. It's difficult to estimate how many little children may be involved in this clandestine traffic. Often prostitutes who find they've gotten pregnant in the line of duty will sell their inconvenient progeny at birth. If the baby turns out to be light-skinned or white, it may be worth a lot of money, upwards of $10,000 in some cases. Sometimes older children are snatched to be sold for sexual use to pedophiles or hebephiles. There are reports of an actual auction held in Baltimore a few years back in which adolescent boys were sold to the highest bidder. Many of these kids were already prostitutes and some were reportedly vying with one another to see who could bring the highest price.

## MOBILE MURDERERS

It is unknown, at this point, whether Adam's abductor sexually assaulted him before murdering him. In any case, the murderer seems not to be a pedophile so much as a psychopath—a person who is so divorced from human feelings that he can kill without a twinge.

A particular strain of psychopath is the footloose vagrant sort who wanders from state to state killing people as he goes. These mobile murderers (also called serial murderers or recreational killers) have been extremely hard to catch because there's been no central point where information about them can be stored and analyzed. For more than a dozen years the Behavioral Science Unit at the FBI Academy in Quantico, Virginia, has been perfecting techniques for "profiling" various kinds of criminals, with special emphasis on sexual homicides and serial murderers. In developing these profiles, which often help baffled local police solve crimes they might otherwise have no luck with, the FBI pays very close attention to autopsy reports as well as maps and photographs of the crime scene. Did the killer bring his own weapon? If so, he was probably a stalker, what is called the "organized nonsocial" killer, a methodical, cunning individual who can charm you to death. Did the killer grab whatever weapon was handy? He might be a "disorganized asocial" type, usually a less intelligent guy, a loner, often paranoid. This type usually strikes once, like the gunman who killed men, women, and children at a McDonald's restaurant in California in 1984. Such an attack, says Robert Ressler, one of the FBI's premier psychological profilers, is very hard to prevent, since there's seldom much forethought. The organized killer, however, will strike many times, always carefully covering his tracks. If you can figure out his pattern, you may be able to intervene and catch him. Wayne Williams, who was tried and convicted for two of the twenty-nine killings of youngsters in Atlanta, would fit this pattern.

When you've got an "organized" killer who travels from state to state, you've got a real problem, since local police can generally not detect the pattern. On April 4, 1981, for instance, the mutilated body of Kathy Whorton, age nineteen, was found in Monroe, Louisiana. On April 14, 1981, Shirley E. Ogden, age fifty-eight, a transient, was found slain in an alley in Jacksonville, Florida. On July 27, 1981, Adam Walsh disappeared from a shopping mall in Hollywood, Florida. The police in Monroe, Louisiana, had no way of connecting Kathy Whorton with any other homicide. Much later, two men were charged with her murder: an amiable-sounding, one-eyed drifter named Henry Lee Lucas, and his gap-toothed, balding, degenerate-looking lover, Ottis Elwood Toole. They'd met back in 1976 outside a soup kitchen in Jacksonville and fell in with each other. In 1980 the two drifters were joined in their travels by thirteen-year-old Frieda Lorraine Powell, Toole's retarded niece. Lucas had a special feeling for the girl and says he never laid a finger on her sexually until she was fifteen. But not long after they became lovers they had a lover's quarrel, during the course of which Lucas apparently dismembered her.

Lucas and Toole, in separate prisons on different

charges, began confessing to murders in various states over a period of years. Dozens of murders. Then, it seems, hundreds of murders. Lucas, particularly, seemed to brag about his exploits, and he may in fact have added a great many that he didn't do. "I've got thirty-six states and three different countries," he told a reporter for ABC's "20/20." "My victims never knew what was going to happen to them . . . knifings, strangulations, beatings; and I've participated in actual crucifixions of the humans. All across the country there are people just like me sent out to destroy human life."

Lucas may be wildly exaggerating his exploits, but he's right about there being others who are bent on destruction. Some estimate there may be thirty-five serial murderers right now driving around the country, committing mayhem and then driving on, leaving the baffled police trying to solve what seem isolated crimes. Others say there may be more than a hundred such people.

Lucas claims that he and Toole sometimes killed together, sometimes separately. Kathy Whorton may have been a joint effort, if their account can be believed. Ten days later, in a different state, one or the other of them may have killed a bum in an alley. Then in July 1981, Lucas was picked up for trying to steal a truck. He was in jail in Wilmington, Delaware, when Adam Walsh was kidnapped.

After hinting around several times about something that happened in the Fort Lauderdale area, something that might involve a child, Toole confessed that he had abducted and killed Adam Walsh.

Maybe he did. He seemed to know things about the case that only the killer would know, and yet he couldn't direct police to where the rest of Adam's remains were supposedly buried. Maybe he forgot. Or maybe he didn't do it at all. He did, however, seem upset by the case. Usually, he'd be totally unmoved as he recited his grisly litanies, but this is one crime he didn't want to take credit for. In fact, he tried blaming it on Lucas before the police pointed out the impossibility of Lucas's involvement. And after Toole confessed, it's said there were tears in his eyes. The tall, beefy, dimwitted pyromaniac and murderer seemed actually sorry. A while later, though, he retracted his confession.

Now the FBI has a much better chance than before of solving such crimes. Its profiling skills, honed over the years, are about to be turned into a computer network that will gather and analyze data about homicides all over the United States, picking out similarities and searching for patterns that might indicate the work of a serial murderer. This Violent Criminal Apprehension Program (known as VI-CAP) should be in operation by the end of 1985. It will provide a national clearinghouse for unsolved violent crimes across the country.

It's easy to say this should have been set up ten years ago. If it had been, it's possible Lucas and Toole would have been picked out by computer and found long ago, and Adam might not have been murdered. But the FBI's Robert Ressler doesn't think that criticism is fair. The increasing presence on the scene of multiple murderers is a recent phenomenon, he says: "We're in a new era of violence," and VI-CAP wasn't really needed in the 1960s the way it is now.

The FBI expects some 10,000 homicides to be processed by VI-CAP computers during the program's first year in operation. And that's just a start. Clearly, this new streamlined computer setup is not coming on line a moment too soon.

# 2

## Parents Who Steal Their Children

They made an attractive couple, the raven-haired Gladys Montalvo and her handsome husband, and they had two beautiful daughters. But, as so often happens, the marriage didn't last, and in 1980 the couple divorced. Eight-year-old Monica and five-year-old Sonia stayed with their mother in their Brooklyn apartment. Daddy would come by now and then and take the kids on little outings. A sad but typical story of modern life—or so it seemed on the surface.

Then, one November day in 1980, he picked up the children and never returned.

That made it into another sort of "typical" story: Ex-Spouse Snatches Kids. Between 100,000 and 500,000 parental child-snatchings take place every year. An incredible number, an incredible amount of emotional pain. And the police reaction was also typical. When the children weren't back by nine that evening, Mrs. Montalvo called the police. "They told me that I had to wait at least twenty-four hours," she later related to a reporter. They said they "couldn't really do much, because [the children] were with their father. And they kept saying that he had as much right to have them as I did."

Maybe, the police told her, "he just wanted to punish you."

Nearly fifty hours went by before the police reluctantly began moving on the case. This, in spite of the fact that the absconding ex-husband had left two notes behind in the apartment. "One of them," recalls Gladys Montalvo, "said something to the effect that he was leaving me just as before we met, childless and alone. In the other note, he [asked] God to forgive him for what he was going to do, but he wanted to be with his daughters forever."

Richard Ruffino, a crack missing-children expert and former detective with the Bergen County, New Jersey, police, is appalled. "How could anybody of any intelligence not understand what this man has written? If I found a note like that, I'd have to presume that either these kids are dead or that something tragic is *about* to happen. I'd send out an APB [all-points bulletin] on them. Make sure that the whole country knows that these kids are out there. But what did they do? For three months they didn't enter those kids in the system [the National Crime Information Center computer]. They didn't even put a warrant out for the husband!"

In late February 1981, over three months after the girls had disappeared, the body of little five-year-old Sonia was recovered from the Hudson River. Monica and her father are still missing.

There's a building national consensus about the need to protect children against pedophiles and murderers. But, apparently, nobody wants to know about the ticked-off husband who drives his kids to Vermont to get them away from his Connecticut wife. Even child-abuse experts like Ken Wooden don't think that parental abductions should be mixed in with the general problem of missing kids. "The issues," he says, "have been clouded" by talking about custody disputes as if they were Adam Walsh–type abductions. "It messes up the focus and the national commitment."

It might be tough to tell that to Gladys Montalvo. It is true, though, that most parental kidnappings do not result in murder and mayhem. That doesn't mean they're not serious. Many such abductions are traumatic for the children, especially if they're told (as many are) that the parent they were taken from doesn't love them anymore and doesn't want them back.

Nor can we be sure that they're in good hands. Custody is often denied a parent for good and sufficient reason. Dr. Eugene Evans, a psychologist, told documentary producer Jerry Miller of KDKA-TV, Pittsburgh, that many parentally abducted kids are sexually abused. "Certainly, there's been a huge percentage of physical abuse and emotional trauma."

With nearly half of today's marriages ending in divorce, parental kidnappings are becoming frighteningly common. In fact, the phenomenon is taking on the dimensions of a national tragedy. Yet police attitudes remain what they were. Says Richard Ruffino, "Most law-enforcement people think that parental kidnapping is strictly a civil matter and they have no business being in it. That's not the *law*, though."

The laws, in fact, have improved lately. "If I have custody of my kids and my wife takes them across a state line and fails to return them, I can file for a federal warrant. The FBI would get involved with that now, as a regular kidnapping."

If police reaction time were faster, all that might not be necessary. Sergeant Joseph St. John of the Missing Persons Division of the Indianapolis Police Department has a national reputation for finding *every* missing child whose report comes his way. His secret: jump on the case the minute the call comes in, even if it's three o'clock in the morning. Jump on it and stay on it and solve it. No waiting period.

Parental child-snatchings, he says, are usually resolved fairly simply. The father may be jealous if his former wife starts seeing another man, and he may take the child to punish her. Or he may take the child as leverage to get some concession. "Usually, it's just a matter of going out and talking to him and saying, 'Why don't you bring the child back?' "

Of course, it's not so simple if the parent whisks the child out of state. At that point the FBI's NCIC computer can be brought into play. Good results can also be achieved by bringing in someone like Dr. Ken Lewis of Child Custody Evaluation Services in Glenside, Pennsylvania. When a child disappears and parental abduction is strongly suspected, Ken Lewis will apply to the court for legal guardianship of the child—even though he's never met the child. This doesn't have to do with custody. "But it's just like, if I were a lawyer, the court would appoint me as lawyer for the child."

Once he is made "guardian *ad litem*" (guardian for the duration of litigation), Lewis is the child's advocate, with legal rights. "Now I can get private material, I can travel across the country or across the world with the child, I can get a passport, I can get school records, I can get anything you could get for your own child."

A highly kinetic, can-do personality with an individualistic, Lone Ranger sort of approach, Lewis has handled hundreds of child-snatch cases in the past ten years. He doesn't talk about all his methods, but he does say he checks out the NCIC computer and about fifteen other computer files, including MasterCard, Visa, American Express, U-Haul, the airlines, and so on. "When I go knocking on the door of one of these computer services, I represent the interests of the child"—and they can't refuse him access.

Have court order, will travel.

One of his more intriguing sources is the computer of ARA Food Services, which supplies food for airports, schools, colleges, even the cafeterias in state prisons. One father fled with his little boy to a small Florida town where he got a job washing dishes in the state prison. "His pay-checks came, not from the state, but from Philadelphia, from the headquarters of ARA Food Services. So, running a check on that, they came up with his name."

Once he locates a child he must decide "Do I want to bring him back to the jurisdiction of the court, or do I want to surface the child—freeze the child—where he is? Many times, if it's an abduction prior to litigation, I will freeze the child [where he is] and enjoin the child and the parent from leaving that jurisdiction. But if the abduction comes *after* a court trial, and if the judge remembers the testimony and has talked with the child in chambers, the judge may say, 'I'd like to have the child back here.' "

It gets very complicated. About half the time Lewis will "freeze the child out there somewhere," and the other half, he'll bring him back.

In his experience he's found that there are four basic kinds of parental child-snatches. If you're a parent whose marriage is beginning to feel shaky, you should probably look at these categories carefully, with a view to heading off an abduction before it happens.

### 1. Prelitigation

This is what Lewis calls the "jump-the-gun" category, in which the mother or father decides that the legal system is not the solution. There are a number of reasons one might feel this way. A father may snatch his child before a court hearing because he thinks the legal system won't treat him fairly. He may be convinced that the court has a sex bias in favor of motherhood. A mother, on the other hand, may steal the child because she fears that something in her past will be held against her. "Fear of unfitness," Lewis terms it.

Actually, he says, it is usually the mother who steals the child. It's a "media myth" that fathers snatch kids more often. "Before litigation, when it's just the husband and wife having a fight, Mom usually picks up the kids and splits." If the father steals the child, he says, it will almost invariably be the son. "It's the feeling—*my son*. Real macho. 'She can't raise him right' or 'Her boyfriend smokes dope.' "

### 2. *During the litigation itself*

A custody trial, Dr. Lewis reminds us, "is not Monday morning from nine to ten." It's the collection of hearings on the case. It could last two or three days or two or three years.

What generally happens in this kind of child-snatch is that one or the other parent comes to feel that the litigation process is going against him or her. So it's time to grab the child and go. This type is somewhat less common than the first, but again it is usually the mother who decides to bolt with the kid.

### 3. *As a power play*

This is a more violent category, and it can happen before, during, or after the custody trial. It's like a standard kidnapping case (such as the Lindberg law was written to cover), except that it's committed by a parent or relative. Often there's a physical scuffle.

It's also, according to Lewis, a "more self-centered" act than the first two kinds of snatches. *Those* are often done with the interests of the child in mind. This kind is to get something for oneself.

"Say the mother takes the kid and goes off to parts unknown. Leaves a note on the icebox. And she calls from a hotel somewhere and says, 'I'm going to come back into town and file for divorce and I'm going to sue you for this, that, and the other. You can avoid all that and save your legal expenses; just sign the piece of paper I'm going to send you." Maybe she wants $350 or $400 a month in child support. If he refuses, says Lewis, "she may say, 'Okay, I'll sue you for custody, and you'll wind up paying all this money, and I'll be in charge of the visitation as the custody parent.' "

This sort of thing, says Lewis, "has the same drama, the same motive, as blackmail, except it's in the family." It happens, he says, quite frequently.

### 4. Third-party parental abduction

In many states "parent" is legally expanded to include grandmother, cousin, uncle, sister, stepfather, etc. "Let's say you've got two kids. One's sixteen and the other's nineteen. The nineteen-year-old may be behind it. He may just take his brother out of school one day and say, 'You're living with me. Our parents are having a hard time and I want you away from that.' "

Lewis cites a further example: "The grandmother comes to Thanksgiving dinner, to her son and her daughter-in-law, and she sees marijuana in the home and decides, 'God doesn't like this.' So she takes the child and doesn't return him. She disrupts his school and registers him in the school in the town where she's living."

In that case it's not difficult to locate the child. But sometimes the child's name is changed. That's when you get what Lewis calls "vitriolics." An example: the child's mother and her boyfriend steal the child, run to a different state, and give him the boyfriend's last name.

All four types of child-stealing are likely to have as a common denominator the child's psychological anguish. But each case must be considered separately. About 40 percent of the time Dr. Lewis recommends that his "guardian child" be put in the permanent custody of the person who stole him.

"After the trial is over and I've made my recommendation and the judge finalizes it, we stay with the guardian child for about five years afterward, following the school grades and keeping in touch with both the mother, who may now be the visiting mother, and the father, who may now be the custody father." The idea is to make sure there isn't a "snatch-back" after the original abduction.

Older children, says Lewis, will most often want to remain with the parent who stole them. In fact the original encouragement for the abduction may have come from the child. "I don't want to go back. Don't send me back," he or she may tell Lewis. It's very important in such cases, he says, "that the child doesn't come to view the legal system as [depriving him of] the parent that he's come to love underground."

What we're dealing with are delicate emotional filaments woven into a web of relationships. And in "third-party" abductions, where a brother or an aunt takes the child, things can get even more complex. Such cases often go way beyond simple questions of a parent's fitness or unfitness. They comprise a whole network of relationships in a wide, extended family. It's like Br'er Rabbit's tar baby—the tar baby of reality: you can't touch it anywhere without becoming involved.

## Is Your Child a Candidate
### for Parental Abduction?

If you're divorcing your spouse and have custody:

1. Has there been a bitter fight over custody matters?
2. Has your child expressed a strong preference to be living with your spouse?
3. Is your spouse extremely upset about your contemplated remarriage or your new boy- or girlfriend?
4. Has your spouse suddenly begun showing great attention to your child after having exhibited very little such concern during the marriage?
5. Has your spouse suddenly become very friendly toward you after a long period of conflict? Could he or she be using you to gain greater access to the child?

6. Has your spouse begun exhibiting unstable behavior? One support agency found that 90 percent of the women who contacted them had been beaten before their husbands snatched the kids.

7. Has your spouse changed his or her life-style lately— e.g., new marriage, new job, new home, a move to a new state?

# 3

# *Physical Abuse*

There are no perfect parents. We've all crossed the line with our children at one time or another—slapped when a simple reprimand would have sufficed, perhaps shaken or punched when milder measures would've worked better. No one taught us how to be parents; yet, suddenly, here the children are and we're supposed to be experts on how to raise them. Sometimes the stress can lead to physical abuse, no matter how much we love our kids.

I remember when my own son was an infant. Since my wife had the nine-to-five job in our family, I usually took care of the baby, all the while working on my dissertation, keeping up with the housework and shopping, doing part-time teaching, and writing articles for magazines. There were times when my joy at having this delightful and good-natured child—my first and only—had to compete with an upsurge of bewildered anger that I had no personal freedom any longer, no money, no time to myself, and very few discernible prospects. Once, when the baby would not stop crying, I took hold of him and shook him—a very dangerous thing to do to a young child. I felt horrible about it afterward.

This chapter, then, is for *all* of us. We've all been there, and we can use all the help we can get.

"Physical abuse" means excessive use of force on a child. For our purposes it also means neglect of a child's basic needs.

The key word is "excessive." What is child abuse to one parent might seem appropriate discipline to another. It's generally agreed, however, that punishment that leaves marks or bruises is excessive. Abuse might also be defined in terms of motivation: we're abusing our child if the punishment is a vent for our own anger rather than a technique for correcting the child's behavior. Damage can be done by verbal abuse, too, of course. We may do as much harm when we scream at a child as when we strike him. Actually, it's seldom necessary to do either. Most parents do both. Nearly all feel bad about it afterward.

This last is a good sign. It's important to keep in mind that "child abuse" is a very recent problem—recent because before that it wasn't considered a problem. It was a custom. Under ancient Greek and Roman law, a father had absolute power over his children. They were property that he could mutilate, sell, or offer up for sacrifice. Kids didn't fare much better in China, Peru, Mexico, or India. Abraham, in the Old Testament, is traditionally admired for his willingness to sacrifice his son, Isaac. Nobody checked with Isaac about *his* feelings.

In colonial America, floggings were considered an acceptable form of child discipline; and in Massachusetts and Connecticut, filial disobedience was punishable by death. The Massachusetts Stubborn Child Law, enacted in 1654, reaffirmed (!) in 1971, and finally repealed in 1973, allowed children no right to dissent against the reasonable and lawful commands of their parents or guardians.

A legal challenge to the absolute rights of parents over children was first made in the "Mary Ellen" case in New York City in 1870. A group of church workers appealed to the Society for the Prevention of Cruelty to Animals for assistance in getting a badly beaten and neglected child named Mary Ellen taken from her home. They argued that she was technically a member of the animal kingdom and therefore was due the same protection as any other member of that kingdom. The child was legally removed from the home, and the case led to the founding of the Society for the Prevention of Cruelty to Children in 1871.

With the Social Security Act of 1935, child welfare became a public, not just a private, concern, but it wasn't until 1962, when Dr. C. H. Kempe and his associates coined the phrase "battered-child syndrome," that national attention began being focused on child abuse. Various states then began enacting mandatory child-abuse reporting statutes.

In 1974, Congress finally signed into law the Child Abuse Prevention and Treatment Act, essentially requiring all citizens to report child-abuse cases to authorities. But we have millennia of cruelty to balance against a few brief decades of concern for children's rights, and with the high incidence of alcoholism and drug abuse in this country, there are more out-of-control parents than ever.

The children's rights movement of the 1980s owes more than a little to the successes of the women's rights movement of the 1970s. As Gloria Steinem told me recently, "The woman who's feeling powerless and without alternatives is more likely to be aggressive towards her children, who are the only thing within her power." The slave of the slave, she reminded me, is treated worse than anyone. The further empowering of women should help alleviate the oppression of children.

In the meantime, reform is afoot. Society's conscience and consciousness are being raised. But there are still more than two million children being physically abused in this country every year. They suffer for a variety of reasons. The following nine factors, either separately or in combination, often lead to physical abuse:

1. Ignorance about child rearing. One mother beat her one-year-old baby for not behaving more responsibly. She didn't understand that there are *stages* of child develop-

ment. With increasing numbers of uneducated and unwed teenage mothers in our society, more and more kids are being beaten or dangerously neglected because the parent doesn't know any better.

2. Addiction is an even greater danger. Fifty-five percent of child-abuse deaths occur in homes where one or the other parent is addicted to drugs or alcohol, according to Odyssey House, an international drug-treatment organization. Of these victims 65 percent are infants or toddlers. One New York mother, high on heroin, unknowingly placed a mattress on top of her baby and then lay down and slept for fourteen hours. The child suffocated.

3. Physical illness, particularly a chronic disease, can lead a parent to neglect a child's basic needs. A sick parent may not have sufficient patience to take care of a child. Pain has a way of shortening tempers.

4. Mental illness and retardation can also lead to severe child abuse. One psychotic mother, hearing God calling her baby to join the angels, suffocated the child with a plastic dry-cleaning bag.

5. Related to this is religious fanaticism. One man who lived in a trailer park in Corpus Christi, Texas, thought the devil had taken possession of his child. He exorcized the demon so vigorously that the child died.

6. A much more common problem is the "tradition" in many families to use harsh corporal punishment for even minor infractions of household rules. Children who survive this upbringing have a tendency to repeat the pattern with their own children.

7. Extreme or persistent external pressures can trigger family violence. Often these pressures are financial and can be relieved with some help with budget management. Job stress, sexual problems with one's spouse, dissatisfaction with one's life can all lead to child-beating. Such stresses are found at all economic levels.

8. Culturally transmitted misinformation can sometimes

lead to physical abuse. Some Caribbean islanders are said to believe that a child who isn't toilet trained by eighteen months should be immersed in scalding water.

9. Finally, there's the problem of "emotional deficits," as child-abuse expert Dr. Judianne Densen-Gerber puts it. Some parents are generally immature, lacking in empathy, and dangerously careless about their children's welfare. Indifference can be fatal and is in itself an insidious form of child neglect.

If you don't recognize any of these conditions in yourself or your spouse, you may be in pretty good shape, and your child is probably in good hands. However, it's not enough just to check off a list of "contributing factors" to be sure you're not on it. It's necessary as well to look at the relationship you have with your spouse and the kind of upbringing you've had. One study suggests that women are more prone to commit child abuse if their husbands are physically or verbally abusive to them, or if the women were physically punished by their own fathers when they were adolescents. Men, on the other hand, are more likely to commit child abuse if they've recently moved to the neighborhood and don't know many people; if they've been married less than ten years to full-time housewives and have two or more kids in the home; if they themselves had been physically punished as adolescents by their mothers; and if they grew up in families where the mothers often hit the fathers.

Such studies are not to be received as holy writ, but they're suggestive. Ask yourself, if you're a woman who has occasionally been knocked around by your husband: Do you sometimes feel the urge to pass your husband's slap along to your child? If so, be sure you have contingency plans—a way to get physically away from your child for a brief time and a number you can call (hot line or trusted friend) for support and help. If you and your spouse share many or most of the characteristics just cited, yours may be a "high-risk" family. It's important to find counseling or other help before your children suffer.

## A Quick Checklist for Parents

1. Are there certain "vulnerable" times of day? Child abuse frequently takes place at dinnertime, when the mother may be trying to get dinner together, the child may want attention, and the father is bringing his own problems home from the office. Mornings are another "flash point," when everyone's trying to get out. Be especially careful to maintain self-control during stressful times of the day.

2. Have you scheduled some private time for yourself? No matter how much you love your child, you must give yourself a break, if possible at least an hour, during the day.

3. Does one of your children resemble (or in other ways remind you of) an ex-spouse whom you now dislike? If so, there's a tendency to take out on the child the resentment you may feel for the former spouse.

4. Is one of the children different (weaker, sicker, wilder) than the others? Often there's an unconscious tendency to make one child the target or scapegoat for one's dissatisfactions in life.

5. Do you have a friend or other adult with whom you can let off steam when parenting gets too stressful? If you feel in danger of losing control, keep a local hot-line number near your phone. Most communities have crisis centers that one can call at any hour. Feelings of isolation, of being trapped, are among the strongest danger signals. It's at such times that one's self-control is most severely tested.

6. Do you have a contingency plan for times when you feel you might be losing control? Is there, for instance, a safe, childproofed room where you can put your child for at least a few minutes while you go into a different room and

pull yourself together? You must get physically away from your child at such times. Do you have an arrangement (perhaps reciprocal) with a neighbor, or with your own parents, when such crises come up?

# 4

# Sexual Abuse at Home

"To protect my public persona, to keep my life with Dad from tainting it in any way, I developed a way of relating to my friends that looked warm and friendly but seldom strayed from the most superficial level. I knew instinctively that intimacy was dangerous for me. A close relationship could lead to the revelation of my secret. I became very good at going through the motions; I shared very little of myself."

An inability to relate honestly to other people, the fragmentation of one's personality, and, above all, the sickening feeling of guilt—these are the effects of incest on many children. To the author of the above description, Katherine Brady, in *Father's Days*, the sexual violation was almost secondary to the absolute violation of trust. Making it worse was her inability to prevent it from happening again and again. She was dependent emotionally, physically, financially on her assailant.

And she couldn't talk about it. All she could do was make pathetic, veiled pleas for help. She writes:

Many Saturday mornings, I tried to talk Mother out of going shopping.

"Do you *have* to go?" I'd ask.

"Yes, Kathy," she'd say, irritated by my question and my tone. "I have to get material for your new outfit. We need groceries, and there's a whole load of cleaning to pick up. Of course I have to go."

"Can I come with you?"

"Don't be silly. I can do it faster without you."

"Please, Mother," I'd plead, "I can help. I'll drive the car for you."

"I said *no*, Kathy. . . ."

Sexual abuse in the home is a tough subject for parents to think about. We'd all prefer it if incest were simply a theme of ancient myth: Oedipus marrying his mother. Failing that, we'd settle for incest as an archaic term for certain historical events in the dim past. The wicked Caligula, they say, ravished his sister, Drusilla; but then, what do you expect from such decadent folks?

Unfortunately, the inclination to reach out and touch someone in one's own family has not disappeared with the fall of the Roman Empire. If anything, current statistics suggest that sexual abuse of children and adolescents within the home is on the increase. And it's not confined to the poor, the backward, or the illiterate. Incest tends to be a white-collar crime. The incestuous father is often a churchgoing, hardworking, intelligent guy. He's also a deeply troubled man, but this may not be evident on the social surface. Even his wife may not realize the nature of his neurosis.

That's why we have to talk about it. Even if we feel quite certain that incest is not occurring in our family, it's important to be sure that the conditions that can *lead* to it are not present, either. And we owe it to the other children in our neighborhood to keep an informed eye out for their welfare. It's no longer enough to be our brother's keeper; we must, in a sense, be our neighbor's children's keeper as well.

Incest may be defined as sexual relations between family

members who are so closely connected by blood that marriage between them is prohibited by law. This means, for instance, brothers and sisters, first cousins, fathers and daughters, uncles and nieces, mothers and sons.

Laws differ, and many states have legislated against "intrafamilial" sexual relations, including stepfathers, stepdaughters, and others who, while not connected by blood, share the *structural* relationship of a nuclear family. Sexual incidents between such people could be called "psychological" incest, and the effects can be just as traumatic as the other kind.

Considering the continuing power of the incest taboo in our otherwise permissive society, it may seem strange that those who violate it are almost never punished. Perhaps it is our very abhorrence of the crime that makes us unwilling to admit that it has taken place. But that unwillingness only makes us the offender's accomplice. Since none of us wants to be in that position, we have no choice but vigilance.

States differ widely in their policies on punishment. Judges will often "sentence" the offender to have psychological treatment. If a jail term is mandated, it could vary from ninety days to thirty years. There seems no national consensus on how we should treat incest offenders.

Often what prosecutors will do is ignore the incest laws, preferring to bring charges of "sexual battery," which tend to carry a heavier sentence. In Florida charges of "capital sexual battery" can be invoked if the child is twelve years old or younger. This means that the adult molesting the child can get a life sentence, with twenty-five years the minimum mandatory term to be served. Florida does not take the sexual exploitation of children lightly.

This is assuming the crime is reported in the first place. Most of the time it is not.

And not all incest is equal, apparently. Many people find brother-sister incest less reprehensible than father-daughter incest, and certainly less than the (rare) father-son incest. If a brother and sister are about the same age and are curious about each other's sexual equipment, the resulting incest may not be traumatic to either, primarily because there is no betrayal of trust. However, the greater the age difference between siblings, the more betrayal (and trauma) will be involved. A sixteen-year-old boy who coerces his ten-year-old sister into submitting to intercourse with him is messing up that girl's life, possibly forever. There is no question of consent here, certainly not of informed consent.

Reliable figures are not available, but a recent Cornell University study found a relationship between the victim's age and where the sexual abuse occurred. If the findings are correct (the sample was limited to 177 cases), it means that preschoolers tend to be victimized outside the home and by men under age forty. Sometimes the men are related to the children, sometimes not. By contrast, teenagers tend to be sexually abused at home by a father or stepfather who is between the ages of forty-one and sixty-five. Although these findings don't suggest any specific strategies, it's useful to know where the *main* dangers lie at which ages. The important thing is not to close your mind to the possibility of incest. Many a mother does not see evidence of incest because she is anxious *not* to see it.

## Types of Incestuous Fathers or Stepfathers

Incestuous fathers have strong needs for physical touch, and they often don't know how to be affectionate in nonsexual ways. Four basic types have been identified. Do you recognize any of these men in your or a neighbor's home?

1. There's the *tyrant,* authoritarian, domineering, fear-inspiring, who may use force or threat of force to make his daughter (or, rarely, his son) submit to him. Usually the daughter is starved for affection and approval and will sub-

mit without force being applied. There's also such a power imbalance, both physical and psychological, between them that resistance may seem futile—not to say disobedient. This father is likely to be extremely jealous of his daughter's boyfriends and may outlaw them entirely. He may also severely restrict her other normal social outlets.

2. Then there's the *rationalizer*. He justifies what he's doing by telling himself that he's just expressing his love for his child. He may tell himself that he's teaching his daughter the correct sexual procedures to help her when she goes out in the world to meet boys.

3. The *introvert* makes the family his exclusive universe, his haven from the pressures of outside life. Often ineffectual in his social relationships, the introvert is dependent on family members for everything. And if his sexual relations with his wife deteriorate, he'll turn to his daughter to fill that function.

4. The *alcoholic* incestuous father is a dependent personality who drinks in order to give himself a spurious feeling of independence. Alcohol does several things: it lowers inhibitions, weakens self-control, and later serves as a convenient object of blame. It was not his, but the liquor's fault that he raped his daughter.

All four types have several characteristics in common. Their incestuous acts tend to occur at times of great stress, often at times when the husband-wife relationship is strained. Unable to turn to the wife for sexual solace, such men will turn to their (less threatening) child.

These men, when the incest is discovered, will almost invariably deny that it happened. If denial doesn't work, they'll blame the daughter (who seduced them) or the wife (who drove them to it).

Incestuous fathers, like child molesters generally, are men (and less frequently, women) who "feel powerless and insignificant in the adult world," says criminologist Dr. Georgette Bennett. "And so they feel comfortable with those who are weaker and more vulnerable than they are. I think that's the missing piece—the issue of power."

Often the incestuous father or stepfather will protest that he loves his children, says Dr. William Hobson, who works in the sex-offender program at the Connecticut Correctional Institution in Somers, Connecticut. The therapist working with these men may counter, "Well, if you loved all your children, how come you were sexually active only with your daughter?" It's not easy, says Dr. Hobson, "to tease out of them some of their rationalizations and faulty thinking." They have an emotional investment in *not* getting the point.

## ASSESSING THE DAMAGE

A few researchers, and even some organized groups, argue that incest is not a serious matter and that the taboo against it is a mindless prejudice from the benighted past. But apart from the appalling betrayal of trust that most acts of incest involve, there are undeniable long-term psychological aftereffects. It's been estimated that between 20 percent and 30 percent of mentally disturbed children were at some time involved in an incestuous relationship. Some of these children have even developed multiple personalities. Whether the incest experience caused this personality splitting or merely triggered the development of an already latent tendency is unclear.

What is clear is that incest has ruined many people's lives, making it very hard or impossible for the victim to trust other people again. And unlike other forms of molestation, incest tends to go on for a long period of time. One estimate suggests that more than 70 percent of incestuous relationships last more than one year, and over 10 percent last more than three years. Some cases involve ten years or more of sexual victimization.

And there's also a multigenerational dimension to the

problem. Most incestuous fathers were themselves sexually abused when they were children or they witnessed sexual relations between their own fathers and their sisters. They tend to have been deprived of affection and attention as children, and many had run away from home at an early age. Now their own traumatized children may run away from *them*, carrying the destructive pattern into the future.

## Danger Signs

1. Watch out for changes in your child's behavior. Children often act out sexual traumas in various ways. A young child may revert to bed-wetting, long after that problem had been solved. Or he or she may suddenly have recurrent nightmares. The contents of those dreams may be symbolic of the incest in some way. Or the child, whether adolescent or preadolescent, may develop an aversion to one member of the family and may not want to be left alone with him. Or the child may develop precocious sexual behavior. Or she or he may suddenly start doing poorly in school after having done well in the past.

2. A mother who remarries and works at night, say, should be alert to the quality of the relationship that develops between her husband and her daughter. Many women sense that there's something not quite right, but they deny this feeling. It *couldn't* be, so it isn't. Don't deny any feelings you may have. Explore them.

3. A mother should be concerned, too, if she finds herself feeling jealous of her daughter. She may unconsciously suspect that something's going on between the daughter and the stepfather. The mother should try to face and analyze these feelings, if only for the daughter's sake. It is her duty to protect her child. Very often a mother will blame the victimized daughter for the incest when it is finally revealed. This is the ultimate betrayal, of course, for the

daughter, who has a poor self-image to begin with and is already feeling guilty.

If you sense anything like these dynamics in your family, stop and think about what's going on. Keep open the lines of communication with your child.

4. Be concerned if your husband or boyfriend takes an inordinate interest in your daughter's menstrual cycle, if he prohibits her having male friends her age, or if he and she spend a lot of time alone together. Find out what's happening. If your fears are confirmed, act. A call to your state's child-protection agency would be a good first step. Later, the local chapter of Parents United might provide useful therapy for everyone involved.

# 5

## Sexual Predators

The fact that you're reading this chapter—reading this book at all—shows your commitment to protecting your child. It cannot be easy to contemplate the sexual prowlers who choose defenseless children as their prey. I myself have found it difficult to write about them. I don't like this subject. I can't make it a "good read." What you're looking at is my third attempt at this chapter.

We're in this together.

We're in it because we have a common enemy. Knowing that enemy, how he operates, the kinds of kids he singles out, can help us shield our children against him.

Pedophiles, these people are called. People whose primary sexual orientation is to children. Not teenagers, but children, from toddlers to twelve-year-olds. Those attracted primarily to teenagers are sometimes called "hebephiles." We cannot condone the actions of the hebephile, but most of us can't even *understand* the behavior of the true pedophile. We're as bewildered as we are revolted by one pedophile's description of a seven-year-old girl: "She was a little sex kitten . . . she seemed to ooze sensuality."

This man is obviously someone extremely dangerous to children.

## TYPES OF PEDOPHILES

Two basic categories of pedophiles have been established.

1. The *fixated pedophile,* as the name suggests, is a man who is emotionally arrested at an early developmental stage and is sexually obsessed with children who are at that same stage. One study found that 81 percent of sex offenders at the Connecticut Correctional Institution had themselves been molested as children. Some people theorize that fixated pedophiles simply stopped growing, psychosexually, at the age when they themselves had first been molested. (This has not, however, been proved.) These offenders are likely to be unmarried and to have little social or sexual contact with people their own age. They feel like children and are most comfortable in children's company. Their social behavior tends to be childish and immature.

They also tend to be sexually drawn to little boys. This doesn't mean they're homosexual, although some pedophiles hide behind the flag of gay rights. They aren't interested in having sex with men; the obsession is with children. Fixated pedophiles are the most difficult to change. In fact, some penologists feel that their behavior patterns are impervious to psychiatric treatment. Many psychiatrists, naturally enough, disagree.

2. The *regressed pedophile,* on the other hand, is basically attracted to people his own age, and he may turn to children only occasionally, in times of stress. His pedophilia is sometimes a substitute for the adult relationship that he craves but is unable to handle. The regressed pedophile usually prefers little girls to boys, and psychiatrists consider the prognosis much better for him than for the fixated pedophile.

It's dangerous to generalize, however. Many pedophiles, whether "regressed" or "fixated," are content with what they are and even convince themselves that they're helping children, not hurting them. "What we do is we tell ourselves lies," one imprisoned fixated pedophile told me recently. "We tell ourselves, well the kid is doing it with his friend anyway. I'm not hurting him. He's not going to turn into a homosexual. I'm only trying to be a buddy with him. Pure bullshit."

This man is trying to change. But thousands of unrepentant pedophiles band together in support groups like the North American Man-Boy Love Association (NAMBLA), or the notorious René Guyon Society, whose motto is "Sex before eight, or it's too late." They wave the banner of sexual liberation in an effort to dignify their atrocities. These are very dangerous people.

## How Pedophiles Operate

Not only are molesters dangerous, they are also clever and determined. Often they seek out others of their own persuasion to trade information, pornographic photographs, even victims. They keep in communication through an extensive underground network. They send one another letters detailing their conquests, whether real or imagined. They circulate mimeographed newsletters. There are even several manuals on how to pick up children.

One "how-to" author strongly suggests meeting the parents first. "Try to involve yourself in various organizations, social, civic, church, hobbies, whatever. . . . You likely will meet their children eventually."

Another of the author's admonitions is particularly revealing of his own psychology. "Be prepared at any time for Turn Around. It can occur when you least expect it. One day Cheri Lynne [a six-year-old] wrote me a love note and allowed me to fondle her as she rode piggyback. The next day she told her mother she didn't want to see me again.

After sixteen years, the memory is still like a knife turning over and over in my heart. It was the closest I came to suicide." Murder and suicide are not always far apart. Fortunately, the writer seems to internalize his torments, rather than transfer them to his victim. With a slightly different personality, the knife might literally have turned in Cheri Lynne's heart.

Later in his tome the author reveals that he encountered "Turn Around" with *every one* of his victims. Even where there's no actual rape, but only a warm (and possibly pleasurable) rubbing and fondling, it's still way beyond the child's psychological developmental stage and can cause long-term emotional disturbances.

As to the apparent ease with which molesters can gain access to children, another of this "how-to" author's observations is suggestive: "Very few adults take the time and effort to be a friend to a child, and lonely children sincerely respond to one that does."

It's true. And pedophiles manage to have all the time in the world to listen, to ingratiate themselves, to gain the child's trust (which of course they then betray). Theirs is a lifelong obsession, and they have incredible patience. One sentence from the "how-to" manual sticks in my mind: "I knew Gloria's mother before [Gloria] was even born." He had, in other words, begun stalking his prey before the victim even existed.

Divorced women with young children are particularly vulnerable to the blandishments of these often charming men. "In fact," says Robert Derbyshire of the National Center for Missing and Exploited Children in Washington, D.C., "in many cases, pedophiles get married to women with children in order to have access to the kids. When the children reach a certain age, the pedophile loses interest and the marriage will break up. Then he'll go and find another woman to have access to *her* children. A lot of times the mother doesn't suspect."

And often the children will not tell. The molestation becomes a secret between victim and offender, something "just between us." Toys, treats, and other favors may bribe a child into silence; in other cases, physical threats may be used. The child might also be convinced of her or his complicity and made to share the guilt. It then becomes something to hide from Mama. In most families talk about sex is not easy between parents and children; often, the most a child can do is send vague signals, which parents may not pick up on, perhaps because they're not really listening in the first place.

## CHILD PORNOGRAPHY

By some estimates, child pornography is a $2- to $3-billion business worldwide and represents 7 percent of the pornography sold in the United States. Most pedophiles who photograph their little victims in kinky poses are, however, doing so for their own gratification. They also use the pornography as a seduction aid. "Look, Susie, these kids are doing it and, see, they're smiling. So there's nothing wrong with it." When combined with other inducements (like a pretty new toy) and with emotional assurances of love, pornography can often be an effective seduction tool.

A long-overdue federal law signed in 1984 outlaws all forms of photographic exploitation of children, and even removes the obscenity requirement. It no longer has to be proven that the child is actually engaged in a sexual act. This crackdown is helping to stem the flood of child pornography that's been pouring in from Holland and Denmark for decades. Yet Tom Rogers of the Indianapolis Police Department's vice squad thinks the problem is increasing. "There's a crackdown, but there's also more people being involved. Or at least more people getting caught."

The child-porn network, always clandestine, is becoming

even more secretive. "An average person," says Rogers, "couldn't find child pornography. . . . In the earlier days, people actually advertised in magazines, and a lot of child pornography [could be located] through directories." Such directories are quite rare nowadays. The legal dangers are too great.

Not everyone is pleased. "Viewing the photograph of a naked child is a substitute for viewing a child directly," writes the author of a mimeographed book on how to pick up children. "Rather than arousing a child-lover to molest a child, the photograph serves as the focus for fantasy and sublimation and reduces the frustration level that might lead to overt action."

The how-to author is something of an authority on child molestation, having made a study of it all his adult life. He is a pedophile. Like most pedophiles, he's also a "collector." Photographs, videotapes, magazines, 8-mm and 16-mm films, slides, and paperback "novels" are the icons of his furtive religion.

He is also talking through his hat. An estimated 80 percent of "collectors" are active child molesters.

Most prized are the molester's own photos of young kids, if possible in sexual situations. Such photos serve as keepsakes, perhaps because, unlike actual kids, photographs never grow up into adults. The little victims remain, like Peter Pan, fixed forever in time.

Then there are the printed magazines. Still openly available are nudist magazines showing families cavorting in the sunshine. Although such publications seem as lacking in eroticism as they are in bikini lines, they're viewed differently by pedophiles, who ignore the parents and dwell on the unfledged bodies of the very young.

Another class of publication aims at "hebephiles," those obsessed with early pubescent nymphets. Magazines like *Pantied Young Bottoms* carry the disclaimer that all "models" are eighteen or over: "Proof on file." That may or may not be true, but the girls are all outfitted in childish bows and posed with stuffed animals and other infantile paraphernalia.

The supply of very young models for sex magazines is almost limitless. A few are abducted children who are forced to participate; a few are children of unscrupulous parents who want to make extra money. But most are runaways, perhaps already broken in to prostitution, who are willing to do some photo sessions for very little money. They don't realize that before long their faces and budding figures will be seen nationwide in underground magazines, films, and videotapes, and that their exploiters will probably become rich as a result.

## Child Prostitution

Most child prostitutes are recruited from the ranks of runaways. It happens very quickly. A charming, streetwise, protective kind of guy, often a teen himself, befriends the frightened runaway, takes him in, feeds him some nice hot meals, introduces him to drugs, and seduces him. Or her, of course. Traditionally, young girls have been targets for prostitution but, increasingly, young boys have been in demand.

It's essential to make the child feel grateful and obligated. When he's been broken in to sex, and perhaps made dependent on drugs (though that's not always necessary), it's time to introduce him to a "friend," who may be a man of, say, forty. This is the pimp. He, too, is smooth and charming. As child-search expert Patrick Mulligan observes, "A good social worker and a good pimp share a lot of skills." Both will communicate sensitively with the child and show "a responsiveness to where the child is at that particular time."

Soon the time arrives when debts start being called in.

The kid must do something to earn his or her keep. The only thing of value that the child has to offer is his body. That will do just fine.

The child may be started out on the street, learning to lure sexually susceptible businessmen into nearby hotels, or perhaps into a dark movie theater for a quick fellatio session. If the "john" has a car, a half-hour drive around the park can net a nimble youngster fifty dollars, of which forty or forty-five may go to the pimp.

Very quickly these children become hardened and offensively streetwise, making it difficult for police officers or social workers to see them as victims. "Say you pick up a thirteen-year-old boy for prostitution," says Robert Derbyshire, "and he tells you to fuck off. . . . It kind of shatters everything you know about how to treat kids."

Many of these children have run away from homes where they were physically or sexually abused. "So they're used to it already, and here they're making bucks for it, okay?"

Derbyshire has found it possible to reach these children by making them understand that they are, in fact, being victimized. At first they will stand up for their pimp, with whom they feel allied. But if the child is made to understand how much the pimp has been gouging him financially, it may be possible to break the bond between them. But the old bond must be replaced by a new, nonexploitive bond, or else the child will simply be further disillusioned and harmed. This takes more patience, resources, and imagination than our child-protection bureaucracy generally can muster.

## CHILD SEX RINGS

Sometimes groups of children are brought together in an organized way for the purpose of molestation and/or pornography and/or prostitution. Such rings may be formed from the ranks of runaways, but this is not always so. Many kids who get involved in sexually criminal activity come from good homes and continue living there.

A study of forty child sex rings showed that almost half the adult offenders used their occupation as the main access route to their victims. There were teachers, a city public-health physician, an engineer, a school-bus driver, a camp counselor, a photographer, a gas-station owner, and a couple of Scout leaders. Skillfully, these men used peer-group pressure, competition, and a variety of material and psychological rewards as inducements. All-boy rings outnumbered all-girl or both-gender rings by about two to one. Boys, it seems, are becoming the more likely victims of pedophiles.

There appear to be three main kinds of child sex rings.

1. *Solo rings.* These involve one molester and his private harem of children. It won't, of course, seem like a harem, just an ordinary house where kids come in and out a lot. Nothing suspicious. Typically, the offender is terrific at organizational skills and is looked up to by his victims, as difficult as that may be for us to accept.

In an article, "Child Pornography and Sex Rings" (FBI Law Enforcement Bulletin, January 1984), Kenneth Lanning and Ann Wolbert Burgess give the amazing example of a pedophile named Ralph who was sexually involved with over fifty local boys. A police raid netted, among other things, Polaroid cameras and film, meticulous ledgers, biorhythm charts, and (a new wrinkle in pedophilia) computer tapes. An obsessive recordkeeper, Ralph had a memorandum book in which he summarized, and graded, his sexual activity with thirty-one of the boys. He recorded which was the youngest (5.26 years), which the oldest (19.45 years), and the median age (10.89 years). He also calculated the average duration of his relationships (2.2 years) and the average number of sex acts per victim (64.48).

Then there was Ralph's computer, which he used in part

as an index to his child pornography collection so that he could locate photographs of specific sex acts.

How did he do it? There were monetary inducements, and alcohol to lower inhibitions, but the key may be in something the kids said after his arrest—that he was "individually concerned with each of them." Add to that Ralph's skill in exploiting the kids' sense of competition and their interest in secret clubs and parentally forbidden activities, and one begins to see how he might have succeeded.

2. *Transitional rings.* Solo rings don't usually remain solo because of the need of pedophiles to communicate with others like themselves. Once they relinquish the relative safety of total secrecy for the comfort of solidarity, pedophiles may start trading photographs of children and end up trading the kids themselves. Such operations, known as transitional rings, comprise a network of child molesters and "collectors."

3. *Syndicated rings.* This third type of sex ring is highly structured. It recruits children, produces pornography, and delivers boy prostitutes to an extensive list of customers. Usually there are a number of adults involved in running the organization. There may also be underworld connections, although this is not always the case. Of the three types of rings, this is the only one that's run primarily for the money rather than for the thrills.

## Is Your Child Vulnerable to Pedophiles?

All children are vulnerable, but there are certain danger signs to watch out for in your child. According to one study, child pornography victims share many of the following characteristics:

1. They're between ten and sixteen years old.

2. They tend to be underachievers in school, mostly because of inattention and lack of motivation.

3. They spend much of their free time in shopping malls and other places and are often alone.

4. They do not generally come from families that instill strong moral or religious values. They haven't been taught to distinguish between appropriate and inappropriate behavior, or what used to be called right and wrong.

5. They may also come from homes where their quest for love is rebuffed by inattentive or overworked or irascible parents.

6. They have low self-esteem combined with a very great need for affection.

A child who has more than a few of these characteristics is a child at risk. The predators in our midst have a well-trained eye for such vulnerable kids.

## Do You Know a Pedophile?

Among the men who are in frequent contact with your child, keep an eye out for the following:

1. The man does not have (and as far as you know has never had) a satisfying long-term relationship with someone his own age. The more you learn about him, the more alone you realize he is.

2. If you're a woman with young children and you've married this man, ask yourself some hard questions about the nature of your relationship with him. Some pedophiles marry women to have access to their kids. Often the woman develops a gut feeling that something is wrong, but she may refuse to admit to this feeling. Go with your feelings.

3. If a man without children always shows up at children's parties or hangs around playgrounds, he may be just a good-hearted fellow who likes kids. Or he may have ulterior motives. Don't assume the worst—but stay alert.

4. If a man seems just too good to be true—loves being with the kids, volunteers to baby-sit, wants to take them on

trips, and to the movies, to the beach, to the moon—he may *indeed* be too good to be true.

5. If your child suddenly has an aversion to a man whom he or she used to be fond of, find out why. Talk with your child calmly, and listen carefully.

# 6

## *Running Away*

Most children have, at one time or another, thought about running away from home. I gave it a brief try myself, when I was eight years old. I was the "baby" in my family, and my two brothers, three and four years older than I, were almost constantly fighting. I hated witnessing those fights, which usually escalated from jeering to punching and kicking; yet, oddly enough, I felt left out at the same time. The fierce sibling rivalry between my hyperkinetic brothers was also a bond, an intimacy from which I was excluded. It seemed that the only time they paid attention to me was when they took time out from their warfare to zing me with a barb of ridicule for my "babyish" ways. I was made to feel stupid, clumsy, weak, unloved.

And, of course, since my brothers were viewed as "difficult" and "troubled," they seemed to get all my parents' attention. I was the good one. I wasn't allowed to have problems. My harassed and overworked mother depended on me to be the "one ray of sunshine" in her stormy household.

It was with a real sense of anguish that, one morning at dawn, I packed my little suitcase with really important things (including my teddy bear) and slipped out the second-floor window. My oldest brother, on his way to the bathroom, caught sight of my tear-stained face, my suitcase, my baseball cap perched on my head, and he seemed stunned, as if seeing me for the first time.

"What are you doing?"

"I'm running away!" I shot back and in a flash was out on the roof.

He ran after me, banging his head on the window as he tried to reach me.

"Wait up!" he called.

But I was already grabbing the drainpipe, ready to shinny down.

"Hey!"—he tried to laugh—"hey, stop!" He was on the roof now trying to grab me, but too late. I was down in the yard and running. I caught a glimpse of him, standing there on the dew-wet roof in his pajamas, and heard him calling out, "Why?"

Why, indeed. All the elements were there—the low self-esteem, the sense of being unloved, and above all the feeling of being *unseen*. My brief escapade lasted only a day, and I see now that its purpose was to get everyone's attention. In that I was typical of most kids who run away; and in that I was also temporarily successful. I still treasure in my heart the undisguised relief on my brother's face when, toward evening, I stepped out from behind a tree and revealed that I was still alive.

Statistics are unreliable, but over a million kids every year run away from home. Most of them are back within a day or two, but many tens of thousands disappear for long periods of time. Your child could be one of them. You need to know what that means, what kinds of kids are likely to "book out the back door," as they say, and which kids are not. You also need to know what they face, what it's like out there, a child on the street.

I didn't stay away long enough to find out. But as Sergeant Bernard Poggioli can tell you, it can be tough on children. Poggioli runs the Youth Services Unit in New York

City's Port Authority bus terminal. His job is to coordinate three two-man teams, each consisting of a plainclothes police officer and a social worker, who patrol the Port Authority complex looking for runaway children. The idea is to intercept them as they step off the bus and to prevent them from getting out on the street. Once they've been outside awhile, sleeping in doorways or in subways or on rooftops, they seldom come back in again. They become what's called the "street homeless." Or else streetwalkers. In 1983 some 2,800 kids passed through Poggioli's office; 1,100 of them were runaways, most from the five boroughs of New York City. Contrary to popular myth, runaways seldom run very far. They tend to head for the nearest large city. New York, Chicago, Fort Lauderdale, Los Angeles, and San Francisco are particular magnets.

New York's Times Square area—"the Deuce," as it's called on the street—is a predatory place, a frightening netherworld of cheap bars, porno movies, video arcades, adult bookstores, and a cast of thousands of down-and-dirty-looking characters with a lingo and subculture all their own. Drug dealers, transvestites, "chickens" (adolescent boys selling their bodies), "chicken hawks" (pederasts with money to spend), alcoholics, former mental patients, all cast watchful eyes on the passing tourists. It's hardly a place for a child, yet for runaways it holds the attraction of a secret hideout, a Br'er Rabbit's briar patch, where their families can't reach them.

But the odds quickly catch up with them, even if their parents don't. "When they get caught up in the street subculture," says Poggioli, "they physically deteriorate, and their mental condition goes with it." Even if kids don't get into prostitution in a formal way—with a pimp and a participating hotel—many learn to barter their bodies for a place to spend the night. "We've had kids in here with second- and third-stage syphilis at twelve or fourteen years of age."

But Poggioli's options are limited. Running away from

home is not a crime; it's what's known as a "status offense," an act that would not be an offense if the person were of legal age. A decade ago runaways who could not be immediately returned home were held in a detention facility with the general prison population. "But our illustrious lawmakers," scoffs Poggioli, "instead of finding some sort of *middle* ground, went completely the other way." Now, if a child is sixteen, you can't hold him at all. Younger kids are put in a group home, a nonsecure facility from which they can easily escape. "We bring them in the front door, they walk out the back."

## TAKING SHELTER

But after a time, when the high of independence has lost some of its glow under the harsh lights of the Deuce, many kids show up at shelters such as Covenant House, founded by Father Bruce Ritter in New York City in 1968. Covenant House calls its New York facility "Under 21," and many of the kids who take shelter there are not strictly runaways. Some are "throwaways," "drift-aways," or otherwise unwanted children. Two thirds of Under 21's kids are boys, and all but 15 percent are nonwhite (59 percent black, 26 percent Hispanic). In the 1983–84 fiscal year, the shelter took in 12,800 kids. That's a "duplicated" figure, meaning that some children came back more than once. The "unduplicated" figure was 7,100—over seven thousand kids in one shelter in one city in one year. An estimated 20,000 children in New York City are homeless.

Most of Covenant House's kids have seriously considered suicide at one time or another. According to Father Bruce Ritter, fully one third of the girls and one sixth of the boys there have actually attempted suicide at some point in their brief lives. An estimated 82 percent of the residents suffer from extreme depression or other psychiatric problems.

Other statistics: 50 percent of the kids at Under 21 were victims of repeated physical abuse; 25 percent of the girls admit to having been raped; 75 percent of the children come from broken homes, usually well below the poverty line.

A runaway child is a missing piece from a very complex puzzle. He can be tough and wary and at the same time very much a child, starving for love. Whenever possible, Covenant House tries to reunite kids with their families. "If a kid's fifteen and is not claiming he came from an abusive home," says young Peg Glauber, an administrator at the shelter, "then he needs to hear that sooner or later we have to talk to Mom. We just do. We'd do that eventually without their permission, but we'll try for the first two days to get it. Parents have rights too."

Everyone has rights, and everyone is hurting, and no two cases are alike. Each child has a story.

THE STORY OF LITTLE BEAR

There is, for instance, the solidly built sixteen-year-old whose nickname on the street is "Little Bear." With his cocoa-colored skin and round face on the fringe of its first mustache, Little Bear is the sort of hard/soft, tough/easy boy that a girl his age would find cuddly but a street opponent would find dangerous. His hair is short, slicked back, the kinks tamed to tight waves. He has agreed to talk, but he comes in like a prisoner who's been advised of his rights. At first he speaks hardly at all and so softly that it seems he doesn't want his words to be heard.

Asked where he grew up, he looks confused. "Everywhere," he murmurs.

He spent some of his early years in Germany, where his stepfather was stationed. His real father, his mother told him, was killed in Vietnam, but Little Bear doesn't believe anything his mother tells him. Not after she betrayed him. Not after she gave away his brother.

"My mother gave him away when he was born, 'cause she said we were both bad kids. But I used to see him sometimes, up until I was six and he was four. . . . The last day, when they made me and my brother separate, I'll never forget it. Never! I cried for six hours straight. Couldn't nobody stop me."

Later, with the advent of adolescence, Little Bear got into a series of scrapes, including an arrest for shoplifting. In the fall of 1983 he was sent "home" alone to the United States. No one met the plane.

An uncle in the New York area put him up for a while, but soon the boy was getting in trouble again, "jumping turnstiles [in the subway] with weapons on me." Weapons. The boy was fifteen at the time.

For several months he lived out on the New York City streets, all the while continuing school. In the afternoons, after classes, he'd hang around with his friends in the school yard. Then, from 3:30 till 6:00, he had a part-time job in a grocery store, after which he'd hang out with his friends some more, "until everybody had to go home, around 11:00 or midnight." But he had no home to go to.

It was cold in March, he says, "so I stayed on the subway in the nighttime, riding from one end to the other and trying to sleep. The trains I took most was the F train and the GG, 'cause they don't make you get off.

"In the morningtime, I went to a friend's house, got my clothes, took a shower, and went to school. I still went to school, but I didn't finish ninth grade. I got to go back again. But the only way I'm going to win the battle with my mother is to go to Job Corps, so that comes first."

The battle with his mother's been going on all his life, but it reached an acute stage when she returned from Germany, settled near Memphis, and decided she wanted her son to come south and live with her. He flatly refuses. He likes his independence now, has found a girlfriend, and wants a job and an apartment of his own in New York.

In some ways Little Bear's situation is unique; in others it's heartbreakingly typical, and parents who worry that their children may run away from home should warn them what's involved. Runaways in their early teens are entering a legal no-man's land and probably *won't* find the freedom they assume is awaiting them. Not yet legally emancipated, boys of Little Bear's age aren't allowed to get their own apartments or hold jobs without their parents' written approval.

Runaways are also entering a psychological no-man's land of intense, desolating loneliness that can have lifelong effects. Little Bear, for instance, has turned into an unnervingly quiet, withdrawn boy. "Even the girls here [at Covenant House], they say 'Why you never say nothin'?' But it's good to be quiet and stay by yourself. You stay out of trouble that way."

The legal hassles and psychological isolation are made worse by physical conditions: the flat-out poverty and vulnerability to attack and exploitation. In his few months on the street, Little Bear's been conned, jumped, knifed, propositioned. And *he* knows something about self-defense. A naive, middle-class kid just off the bus from Youngstown might not stand much of a chance.

The one hopeful note in the story of Little Bear is his angry determination. "I'm going to make it. I'll go to Job Corps and get me a job, and then I'll be a foster parent."

A what? Yes, one day he'd like to adopt a little boy, maybe four years old. As it happens, that's the age his brother was when last seen. He sees it as his way of breaking the cycle of vagrancy and aimlessness.

Sergeant Poggioli agrees that the pattern can become so deeply established that it seems impossible to break. "We had a thirteen-year-old girl in here the other day," he says, "who's seven months pregnant. Tell me where that kid's going to be? Thirteen years from now that thirteen-year-old's thirteen-year-old is going to be in here too!"

What we're talking about is the destruction of childhood. Little Bear's struggle to survive and prevail, for instance, has not left much room for childish pleasures. Yet now and then childhood's private magic can be discerned, even among street-hardened kids. Because, ultimately, they *are* kids still.

"We had two young girls in here one time," says Sergeant Poggioli. "They were both working the streets. And all of a sudden they open up their pocketbooks and they take out a couple of dolls."

The sergeant shakes his head wonderingly. "They were sitting in here, like little children, playing with their dolls!"

## Could Your Child Be a Runaway?

1. Is your child subject to frequent corporal punishment? Many kids reach the point where it no longer seems worthwhile putting up with the misery.

2. Has your child suffered sexual abuse at home? Running away can literally seem the only escape.

3. Do you have violent arguments with your child? Failure to communicate—or to respect one another's divergent life-styles—can make running away from home seem an attractive solution.

4. Do you have trouble letting your child know that you love him very much? A child who feels unloved will also feel unlovable, develop a poor self-image, and perhaps decide to "go off into the night." A happy, confident child is very unlikely to run away.

5. Has your child been increasingly depressed and uncommunicative lately? Does he have problems that he cannot talk to you about? Does he frequently stay away from home or in various other ways let you know he wants to live

somewhere (anywhere) else? This is particularly likely to happen during the stressful period of adolescence.

6. If you're divorced has your child often expressed a desire to live with the absent parent rather than with you?

7. Are there significant economic problems in your household (with concommitant stresses, such as over-crowding), and has your child come to feel that he's a financial burden?

8. Has your son or daughter run away before, or threatened to run away? Were you or your spouse runaways yourselves when you were kids? Sometimes, running away from home develops into a chronic (even multigenerational) pattern. Certainly, if the reasons your child ran away the first time have not been thoroughly explored and resolved, there is a good chance the child will run away again.

## PART TWO

# Strategies for Protecting Young Children

# 7

# *The Way We Talk to Children*

Even a very small child is a person, someone with rights. Yet it's hard for many parents to think of their little children as actual, fully dimensional people with their own separate and legitimate view of the world. The common assumption is that we must tell them what to do because we know and they don't.

In talking with kids about the dangers of abduction and being hurt in various ways by grown-ups, there are a couple of problems with relying on an authoritarian approach. First, kids don't listen very attentively when they're being told what's good for them and what's not, and this is one time when we want them to listen very carefully indeed. Second, there's something contradictory about our coming on as all-knowing adults when a major part of our message is that adults can't always be trusted. We must even give our kids permission to lie to adults under certain circumstances. Sometimes, they should defy or run away from adults. One of a child's inherent rights, for instance, is to say "No" to a grown-up who touches or talks to him in a way that makes him feel uncomfortable. As Linda D. Meyer notes at the end of her child-safety booklet *Safety Zone*, "By teaching our children to always respect, trust and obey adults, we are inadvertently setting them up for abduction and/or assault. . . . We need to show them that there are also times and situations when we *want* them to question authority, when we *want* them to disobey big people. We need to teach them common sense and problem-solving skills."

In a real way this means making them more independent. But they can never attain independence as long as we persist in thinking of them as cute little pets attached to umbilical apron strings. To protect our small children we may have to revise our parental relationship to them, loosening up those apron strings in some respects while in other ways keeping a closer watch on the children than ever before.

This double action—teaching our children to say "No" and even to lie at times, while increasing our supervision of them—requires us to do as much work on ourselves as on them. And once is not enough. As Kenneth Lanning, a special agent at the FBI, puts it, "What a lot of people don't understand is that protecting your children is not something that you do one evening for a couple of hours. It's something that you do twenty-four hours a day, every day."

Some of the information in the chapters that follow is for parents to impress on their kids; some is for parents to work on themselves. But the information, by itself, is not enough. It must be communicated in the most effective possible ways.

You don't want to terrify your children and give them nightmares; but you don't want to "undershoot" your message, either, presenting it so nonthreateningly that it doesn't sink in. A lot depends on your own personality and the sort of relationship you have with your kids. Ordering, threatening, preaching, advising are generally ineffective ways of communicating with children, as Dr. Thomas Gordon explains in his highly useful book, *P.E.T.—Parent Effectiveness Training*. Such approaches, he says, "communicate to the child *your* solution for him. . . . You call the shots; you are in control; you are taking over. . . . *You are leaving him out of it.*"

As an experiment, sit down with your kids and tell them frankly that you're worried about their safety. You might tell them that most grown-ups like and want to help children, but there are some adults who like to hurt children. Ask them if *they* have any ideas on how they can protect themselves from such people. Make it into a game, and if the children are fairly young have everybody take a piece of paper and write down ideas. Then compare and talk about these ideas.

There are all kinds of approaches you could take. "What if?" games are often effective. "What if you're walking to school and a stranger pulls up beside you and offers to give you a lift?" "What if a grown-up you don't know asks you for directions to the library?" And so on.

Accentuate the *positive* in the children's answers. Don't, for goodness sake, say, "That's a dumb answer, Jimmy." Say, "That's a good idea. Can you think of any *other* ways of dealing with this?"

One approach that works for some parents and teachers is to tell a story to a (fairly small) group of children, and then stop the story at a crucial moment and ask the kids what *they* would do if they were in the predicament that the fictional character is in. Mary Ellen Stone, of King County Rape Relief, in Renton, Washington, often visits schools and talks to children. She told one class of kids from kindergarten through third grade about "Susie," whose neighbor, "Mr. Jones," started touching her in ways that made her feel uncomfortable. "If you were Susie's friend," said Ms. Stone, "what would you do?" The children had lots of suggestions, some of which were off the wall, some right on the mark. Then she told the rest of the story. "She said to Mr. Jones in a big voice, 'I don't want to talk to you any more right now.' Then she went inside and told her mom what had happened. And her mom said, 'Susie, I'm real glad you told me about this. That was an unfair thing for Mr. Jones to do, and I'm going to talk to him and tell him not to do that ever again.' "

The story technique allows an adult to show kids one possible solution to a problem without insisting that this is the only solution. The story in the above example also gives a clue as to a proper parental reaction. Children worry about their parents' reactions and often keep molestation incidents to themselves for fear that their mother or father will get mad or blame them. The story also indicates that something will be done about the incident. Mom is going to talk to Mr. Jones in no uncertain terms. All this is very reassuring to a child.

Role-playing is another effective means of communicating safety messages. "You be the man in the car, and I'll be the boy on his way home." All kinds of surprising things come out of such playacting. A useful part of this technique is that it moves the discussion from the talk level to an action level and hence closer to reality.

Another fun nonverbal way of empowering your children and enhancing their feelings of capability is to enroll them in a martial arts class of some kind, perhaps karate, judo, or aikido, so that they have some options if approached by a threatening stranger. Some parents are afraid of making their little boys into macho bullies and their girls into un-feminine bundles of aggression if they let them have martial training. But that is a myth of the worst kind. Kids love tumbling about on mats, and they love the feeling of having some resources for defending themselves. Aikido, though it comprises only defensive maneuvers, is useful in its incul-cation of centeredness and balance. This in turn brings out in the child a feeling of calm alertness, an awareness of even peripheral objects in the environment. If a child can develop a sense of what's going on around him and even *behind* him, and if his body is balanced and ready to move quickly in any direction, he's a lot better off than a child who is oblivious of his surroundings and unprepared to dodge away from an attack. This has nothing to do with becoming a bully. In fact, as children gain some confidence in their prowess, they tend to become calmer. Our children don't have to be helpless in order to be lovable.

Parents might legitimately worry that their child, even if trained in a martial art, might be ineffective against a molester and that his or her attempts at self-defense would only enrage the attacker. It's true that a half-trained or poorly trained youngster will be ineffective, but a carefully trained child can do some remarkable things. The truth is that molesters are themselves cowardly bullies or they wouldn't be preying on children in the first place. They are often stunned by any show of determined resistance at all on the part of a child and will tend to back off rather than tangle with a little hellcat. There's easier prey to be found elsewhere.

In general, then, whatever your approach, let the motivation be to *empower* your child and make him more savvy and self-sufficient than he is. He or she will love this feeling, so blessedly different from the usual feeling of helplessness in the adult-dominated world.

Naturally, you must keep in mind the age and attention span of the child you're addressing. Really small children have to be given a lot of time-outs as well as a lot of repetitions. The trick is to make safety strategies a challenge for them, something they are a part of, rather than another set of lessons they're supposed to memorize.

# 8

## *Foiling a Kidnapper*

Here's something your child could get actively involved in. Foiling the bad guys, after all, is one of the great childhood fantasies. Have your youngster come up with his own ideas and encourage him to implement them himself. For safety messages really to sink in, children must participate in the process of discovering strategies. Playing "What if?" games can be an engaging and effective way to make this happen. The twenty questions that follow are freely adapted from the *Safety With Strangers* booklet put out by the Adam Walsh Child Resource Center as part of a classroom safety program.

TWENTY "WHAT IF?" QUESTIONS

1. What if you're walking along a street and a man you don't know comes up and says, "Hi, there"? What would you do?

(Among the acceptable possibilities is ignoring the man and continuing to walk on.)

2. What if you're playing with your friends and a stranger comes up and says, "Hey, would you like to come

back to my room? I'll give you some money"? What would you do then?

(This is, of course, a very dangerous situation, but sometimes a child will say that he'd grab the money and run with it. If you get that kind of response, do a little role-playing with the child. Hold a dollar bill in your hand and explain to the child that you're going to try to grab him as he reaches for it. It's very easy to do, and the child will not quickly forget so dramatic a demonstration. Use this opportunity to ask about other possible lures, and do some role-playing about them too.)

3. What if you're walking along and there's a stranger standing beside his car and he says, "Hi. Want to go for a ride in my car?"

(Extremely dangerous, of course. Make sure your child understands just how great the potential for kidnapping is if a stranger is *anywhere near* a car.)

4. Suppose you're walking home. A car pulls up and a stranger calls out, "Get in! Do you hear me? I said get in this car or I'll punch you out!"

(Most kids by now will know to run away and not under any circumstances get in. They should also shout for help as they run.)

5. Another car question: What if you're walking along and a stranger pulls up and says, "Hi, your mom's sick and she asked me to pick you up"? What would you do?

(Children playing this "What if?" game are likely to come up with a variety of possible answers. Be sure they understand that they must *not* go with this person. They might go back inside the school and talk with the principle or a teacher, who will call the child's home to see if Mom is sick or not. Parents should work out contingency plans with their child in case they can't pick him up. If the parent is hurt or delayed, he should call the school and make arrangements for getting the child home. If the child takes a bus home, work out what he should do if he misses his bus one day.)

6. What if you're walking along and a car pulls up next to you and a stranger says, "Excuse me, do you know how to get to the post office?" What would you do?

(Children should understand that grown-ups very seldom ask kids for directions. They ask other adults. The child should go nowhere near the car. Conceivably, the child might shout directions from a distance, or point toward the post office, or say, "I don't know." If the man says he can't hear what the child's saying, it's best just to walk away toward other people and not continue the conversation.)

7. What if you're at a playground and you have to go to the bathroom? A stranger's standing by the bathroom door and says, "Hey, come over here. I want to show you something." What would you do?

(Obviously the child should turn right around and get away from there *fast*. Young kids shouldn't be at a playground by themselves anyway. If a grown-up can't be with them, a close friend should be. And when going to the bathroom, the child should take his friend along with him. In this case he should go back to the other people in the playground and try to find an adult, preferably a woman, and tell her what happened. Almost any man would be perfectly safe to ask, too, of course; but since molesters are practically never women, it makes sense to turn to them first if there's a choice.)

8. What if a car stops next to you and a stranger holds up a cat and says, "Hey, somebody just stole my cat's kittens. Want to jump in and help me find them?"

(Children playing this "What if?" game will probably understand that they mustn't get into the car. They should get away quickly and go into their house or walk toward other people.)

9. What if you're sitting outside feeling sad because your parents have told you you can't play with your friends? A stranger pulls up in a car, shows you some toys, and says,

"Don't look so sad. Come over here and take one of these toys." What do you do?

(Talk with the children about how they feel when they've been punished. Make sure they understand that, no matter how bad they feel, they must never go with a stranger.)

10. What if you're walking down the street and you notice a stranger following you on foot?

(Kids will have lots of ideas about this. Among the more practical: go immediately to where there are other people. If the child's in a store he can go up to a check-out person or other store employee for help. If he's on a street near home he should get straight home or to a friend's house. If he doesn't know anybody on the street and he really thinks somebody's trying to get him, he should ring the first doorbell where it looks as though somebody's at home. At this point discuss with the kids the difference between strangers coming to children versus children seeking help from strangers.)

11. What if you've been playing Frisbee with your friends, and just as you're leaving, a stranger hops off his motorcycle and says, "You sure can throw that Frisbee. Let's take a ride over to my house and I'll show you some special throws"?

(Have the kids talk about how they feel when a stranger compliments them. Get them to explore the idea that people might be friendly in order to get a child to trust them.)

12. What if you're in a video arcade and a stranger comes over and says, "You sure are good at that. Tell you what, let's go to the ice-cream shop next door and I'll get you a cone"?

(Kids will see the similarity with the previous "What if?" They should be cautioned repeatedly not to go anywhere with someone unless they have permission from their parents.)

13. What if you're walking along and a car pulls up? A man says, "Have you seen a black-and-white dog? Mine just

ran away. If you'll get in and help me look for her, I'll give you this dollar."

(Very, very dangerous. And a very powerful triple lure: helping someone in trouble, getting a dollar for doing it, and maybe getting to play with a dog, too.)

14. What if you're in your front yard and a man who lives down the street walks up and says, "Hello, honey, where's your mom and dad? Do you want to come to my house? I've got a new puppy you could play with"?

(This one lets kids think about who a "stranger" is. This man lives on the same block as the child and may even be friends with the child's parents. The point, though, is that even if the child knows the man he should never go with him—especially not into his house—unless the child's parents have given their permission.)

15. What if you're at a pool and a stranger comes up and says, "Hello, there. You're a very pretty girl. You have beautiful eyes"? What would you do?

(Have the kids talk about places where they've been left briefly alone. Skating rinks? Movies? Even in places where a child's parents may be fairly close by, a stranger may come up and talk with him or her. Convicted child molesters have said that they try to find children who are friendly. They get to know a child a bit before the molestation or kidnapping takes place. For young children, it's safer not to talk with strangers.)

16. What if you're at a store and your mother's in the next aisle while you linger in the toy department? A man comes up and says, "I've got some toys just like these at my house. It's just down the street. Your mother won't mind, I promise."

(Almost every kid will see the danger here. But discuss further possibilities with them. Suppose a store security guard comes up and tells them to leave the toy department? What if the guard starts to lead the child out of the store? Children must be trained to speak up to adults. They should say their mother told them to wait in the toy department and they can't leave without her. If the guard still tries to lead the child outside, he should look for some other adult, preferably a woman, and call for help.)

17. What if you're at an amusement park riding the merry-go-round while your parents have gone over to the hot-dog stand? A stranger asks you, "Do you like magic tricks? Come with me and I'll teach you how to do some neat ones to show your friends." What would you do?

(Kids must understand how dangerous this situation is and how important it is not to talk with this man. If their parents told them to wait at the merry-go-round, that's where they must stay. If the man persists, the child should look around for a woman, preferably one with children, and call for help.)

18. What if you're waiting in front of the movies for your mother to pick you up? A policeman parked in front of the theater says, "Your mother's been in a car accident. Get in and I'll drive you to the hospital."

(This is a tough one for kids, because we want them to trust police officers and go to them whenever they need help. But children should know that fake badges are easy to buy. If the officer knows the child's name, and knows the name of the mother, and if the car he's standing in front of is a clearly marked police car, the child is probably safe in believing the officer. If, however, the car's unmarked and the officer doesn't know the child's name, then the child had better look around for another adult. He might ask some grown-up in the theater to help verify the officer's credentials. Any real police officer should be pleased by the child's caution.)

19. What if you're at home alone and a stranger comes to the door and calls out, "Excuse me, there's an emergency. Could I use your telephone?"

(Kids will come up with a lot of ideas, but the simplest solution is to ignore the knock and pretend no one's there. Obviously, if the child can actually see an accident outside, he can call the local emergency number [911 in many areas] for help—without opening the door. Have the kids discuss the whole problem of being at home alone. If there's a phone call for their mother, for instance, they might say that she's in the shower or in the middle of doing something. Or, even better, just say she can't come to the phone now. That way the child won't become confused about which excuse to use. The child should take a message so that the caller doesn't keep calling back. All important phone numbers should be kept next to the phone.)

20. What if you're lost in a shopping mall? A stranger comes up to you and says, "Are you lost? Come with me and we'll find your mom."

(Kids might be confused by this one, but no, the child should *not* go with this man. There are certain rules for shopping malls. Basically, they go as follows:

1. Never go out of the store to look for the car.

2. Never leave the store you are in.

3. Go to a cash register. Look for someone with a name tag and find out if he works there. If so, have him page your parents.

4. If you've lost your parents in the mall but not in a store, stay as close as possible to the place you last saw them, because they're no doubt looking for you. If some time has passed, go into the nearest large store, go to a cash register, and ask the person there to page your parents.

5. If a man grabs you in a store and starts to force you outside, you should scream, "This is not my daddy!" Sometimes parents are seen taking their own screaming kids out of stores, so it's not unheard of to see this happen. That's why it's important to yell that the person who's got you is not your father.)

All this may sound rather alarming, but kids are not "traumatized" by learning about dangers as long as they feel they have an active and creative part in combatting them. That's why "What if?" games and role-playing are so useful: they give children the positive sense that they have at least some control over what happens in their lives.

## A Checklist of Safety Precautions

Going through that "What if?" section at home with your child, or at school with the class, will help suggest numerous strategies for foiling would-be abductors. But remember, once is not enough, and the younger the kids are, the sooner they're likely to forget. In addition, make certain that the following basic safety points are covered:

• Be sure your child knows his full name, your name, and the home address.

• Teach him how to telephone home, and be sure he knows the *area code,* in case he's taken out of state. He should also know how to ask for help from the operator. Practice these things with him.

• Have your child fingerprinted by someone who knows what he's doing (the police, for instance), and keep the only set at home in a safe place. Beware of do-it-yourself kits, by the way, sold by some child-safety hucksters. If the prints aren't taken correctly, they can't be used in the FBI computer.

• Keep copies of up-to-date dental records, medical information, notations of birthmarks, anything that might later be of help in tracking your child down.

• Keep a recent photograph handy and have your child rephotographed every year. If possible, videotape your child as well.

• Get passports for all the children, no matter how young. Once a passport is issued, it's both difficult and suspect to attempt to get another one for that person.

• Tell baby-sitters or day-care personnel that your child is not to go with anybody but you, unless you've given special authorization.

• Be very sure that your child understands that he must never get in a car with a stranger. If he senses that a car is following him, have him run in the *opposite* direction from that of the car—preferably toward a crowd of people.

- Warn your child that a would-be kidnapper may tell lies. Such people often tell kids, "Your parents don't love you anymore. They don't want you home." Sometimes they say, "Your parents are dead. I'm the only one you have." Impress on your child that you love him very much and you always will and that if anybody ever takes him away you'll keep looking and keep looking until you find him.

- Children shouldn't wander about alone. When they're very young, you should be with them. As they grow a bit older and more independent, they should work out a buddy system, so that two or three kids always stick together. There really is safety in numbers.

- Even so, don't let your child play in deserted places, even if his buddy is with him. Some crowded places, like video arcades, are also dangerous. Be sure he goes with (and sticks with) friends that you and he know well.

- Don't put your young child's name on his cap, his book bag, his T-shirt, or other places where it can be easily seen. To do so is to put a would-be abductor on a first-name basis with your child.

- Instead, write your phone number, with area code, inside the tags of your children's clothes. This way, even if your child forgets his number, it's always with him.

- Have a family code word that only you and your children know. If a stranger approaches and wants them to go with him, have your kids demand that he say the family word or phrase. If he can't, they should get away from him fast and call for help.

## LURES AND OTHER TRICKS TO BEWARE OF

Teach your child to recognize and resist any of the following approaches:

1. *The offer of help.* Kidnappers may try to gain a child's confidence by offering to help him with a problem. Fixing

the child's broken bicycle, for instance. The child should say nothing or "No thanks" and move quickly away.

2. *The request for help.* "Say, could you help me carry some of these packages over to my car?" Warn your child that kidnappers are very good at what they do. They're likely to appear quite harmless, disarming, engaging. Ken Wooden, in his useful pamphlet *Child Lures,* suggests that if anybody stops to ask directions or other help, your child should move out of reach, take two steps backward, and be ready to run.

3. *The offer of affection.* None of us gets enough affection, and for a lonely child, the need can be achingly keen. Abductors target kids who stay by themselves a lot. One convicted molester tells how he would ingratiate himself with a child, share his lunch with him, come back several days in a row before making his hit. "You got to gain their confidence. You got to play 'em along, and they'll do whatever you ask."

4. *The exercise of authority.* Impersonating an officer is a crime, but it is certainly effective in making a child come with you. This is very hard to protect your child from, since even adults are often fooled. Abductors may show a badge of some sort or may be dressed as a priest or even a truant officer. We must train our kids to look to another adult—preferably one they know—to corroborate the credentials of whatever authority figure has approached them. *A red flag should go up in the child's mind whenever an unknown adult wants to take him anywhere.*

5. *The sudden emergency.* Children can be easily alarmed, flustered, and tricked by an earnest-looking adult who runs up saying that something terrible has just happened to the child's mother and that he should come with him right away. Again, the child should be trained to stop and think twice whenever an unknown adult wants him to go anywhere. Train your child to get that "second opinion" from a teacher or other known quantity before

doing anything. This is also the perfect time to invoke the *family code word*. If the concerned-looking adult doesn't know it, your child must refuse to go with him. As for the possibility that there's a *real* emergency at home, there could be one, it's true. But the child is not to go with an unknown person to check it out. Work out with your child a special emergency procedure in case something does come up. This might involve calling an agreed-upon neighbor for help.

6. *Joining in children's games.* Alas, children have to be careful of who is playing tag with them. They particularly have to beware of adults who want to play contact sports. Ken Wooden strongly warns about " 'pied piper' types [who] fascinate children with tricks or gimmicks." Try to be with your child when there's some magician or clown entertaining the young troops. Of course, your child will already know to run away if anyone touches him or her in a way that seems wrong.

7. *Threatening the child.* This is a very dangerous situation because of the real danger that your child will be hurt. "Come with me or else!" is the sort of message that should make your child *scream for help and run* in the opposite direction. Impress upon your child that, even if an adult threatens to use force, the child must *not* go with him. Better to take one's chances putting up a fuss out in the open. Nothing good is likely to come of cooperating with a violence-threatening character.

8. *Taking candy from strangers.* Bribery is still a device used by many would-be abductors and molesters. They may offer a child toys, pocket knives, and other gifts and favors. The bribing may go on for a while before an overt sexual move is made; so, as a parent, be alert to any new toys appearing around the house. Find out who gave them to your child. Warn the child not to accept such gifts, but go beyond the vague exhortations that we got as children. Tell your child *why*—not in a terrifying or "traumatizing"

way, but with enough basic information so that he knows what your concern is all about.

## ABDUCTION INSURANCE

With the growing national awareness of the issue of missing children, insurance companies are experimenting with a new category: abduction insurance. Some of these plans are expensive and are designed for the affluent who fear they may have to pay a high ransom if they or a family member is kidnapped. But the field is very much in flux, and those who are interested might contact the Insurance Institute of America in Malverne, Pennsylvania (telephone: 215-644-2100), or the College of Insurance Library in New York City (212-962-4111) for the latest information.

One fairly inexpensive and comprehensive package is offered by the Continental Insurance Company. A four-part Victim Assistance program covers fraud and theft, victim injuries, child abduction, and a family plan that incorporates all of the above. If one wishes one can buy just the child-abduction coverage, called the Missing Child Assistance Plan. It comprises three areas:

1. Kidnapping recovery coverage. Continental will pay for private investigator fees to find any family member under the age of eighteen who's been kidnapped by a stranger. If you use the Pinkerton network, with which Continental has an arrangement, the company will pay all investigative expenses for seventy days in the United States, Canada, and U.S. possessions. The premium holder can call a Pinkerton man on an 800 number the minute his child is missing; there's no waiting period.

If one prefers to use a different detective agency, there's a $250 first-day deductible. For the next thirty days the company will pay a maximum of $500 per day; and for the forty days after that, a maximum of $250 a day. Continental also offers $25,000 in reward money (*not* ransom) for information leading to the safe return of the child, and another $25,000 reward for information leading to the arrest and conviction of the abductor. Plus $5,000 to advertise those rewards.

The company will pay an additional $5,000 in living expenses if one has to travel to some distant point to pick up the child. Another $5,000 is earmarked for medical and/or psychological counseling, if needed, either for the victim or for any member of the family. And $5,000 more is allocated for any other reasonable expenses.

2. Custodial recovery coverage. This part of the plan covers a snatch by a noncustodial parent. In this case the company will pay all Pinkerton investigation fees for seventy days.

3. Supplementary coverage. This includes witness reimbursement fees, in the event that someone has to take off from work or travel a distance to testify at the trial. The reimbursement is up to $50 per person per day, with a maximum total of $2,000. There's also a $5,000 medical allocation for "Good Samaritan" injuries sustained by anyone who got hurt while trying to prevent an abduction from taking place.

As of late 1984 the annual cost of this Missing Child Assistance Plan was under $300, and, as mentioned, it covers all family members under the age of eighteen.

# 9

# *Dealing with a Child-Snatching Parent*

If you're divorcing and are worried that your spouse may be thinking of stealing the children, there are some precautions you can take:

• Know your spouse's statistics. Keep on file, if you can, his or her social security number, date of birth, credit-card numbers, passport number. This will make it easier, if a kidnapping does take place, for the police and/or FBI to track his/her credit purchases, trips out of the country, and other movements. If he has a car, keep a record of the serial number, license number, registration number, and license-plate number. All this may sound paranoid, but if you really have reason to fear an abduction attempt, you should quietly stock up on all the data you can.

• Know all you can about his or her financial resources. The bank he/she uses, the account number, the kinds of accounts, including money markets and IRA's. This information, too, will be of use to the authorities.

• Learn as much of your spouse's personal history as you can. This includes current and previous places of employment, property and other assets, old haunts, hometown, favorite locales.

• Know your in-laws and your spouse's friends and coworkers. Few people drop out of sight forever. Chances are, if your spouse takes your children and disappears, he'll contact some relative or good friend sooner or later. Keep track of the names of these people, as well as their addresses, birth places, telephone numbers, license-plate numbers, automobile makes and years, places of employment, and so on. At the least, this information will give investigators something to go on.

• Before anything happens, take care of custody questions, if you can, so that there's no question as to your legal rights in the matter.

• If custody litigation is in progress, some people advise that you take legal steps requiring your spouse to get permission from the court before going with the child outside the court's jurisdiction. You might explain to the judge that you're afraid of an abduction attempt.

• In divorce papers specify visitation rights as precisely as you can. Try to make it clear when, where, and how long these visits are to be.

• If school-age kids are involved, include in the custody order a provision to prohibit the transfer of school records without your approval. File this with the school.

• With day-care centers, schools, and baby-sitters, make it very clear that your child is not to be released to your spouse without your specific consent. Admittedly, this is a hard precaution to make effective, since many schools and day-care centers don't want to get involved in custody battles. But if they cannot prevent releasing the child, they can agree to call you immediately if it happens.

• Be alert for changes in your former mate's life-style (new marriage, new job, new address), and watch out for noticeable reactions on his/her part to changes you may make in your own life-style (jealousy of your new girl/boy-friend, etc.). There's nothing ominous in any of these things, but be aware of them and try to understand what they may portend.

• Get a passport for your child, however young he may be, and keep it locked in a safe place. If your spouse is thinking of taking the child and settling in New South Wales, it will be more difficult for him to do so if you've got the passport. Keep the birth certificate locked away with it. That will make getting a new passport doubly difficult.

• If your spouse does take the child, crosses a state line, and does not return the child within a short time, remember you have a right to contact the FBI, enter your child's statistics in the NCIC computer, and get a federal warrant issued.

• In the meantime, of course, you will have called your local police. Don't be surprised if they are reluctant to act; they absolutely hate this kind of case. But they're obliged to take it on and pursue it. Keep after them.

• If you're not convinced they're acting vigorously enough, you might contact one of the organizations listed in this book's Appendix that specialize in parental abductions. A private detective is another recourse, but be careful: use only those that are recommended by reliable sources. For general advice, it might be good to contact someone like Dr. Ken Lewis of Child Custody Evaluation Services in Glenside, Pennsylvania.

It's very difficult to prevent a parental abduction, no matter what precautions you take. As Dr. Lewis succinctly puts it, "Children don't resist." If a child is over twelve or thirteen, he says, and does put up a fight, the parent will usually back off, at least for the moment. Such resistance, however, is extremely rare.

Even if a child is reluctant to go, the parent can usually talk him or her into it without causing a scene. "We had a real smart lady the other day," says Dr. Lewis, "who told her nine-year-old boy that Daddy got killed in a car crash and left in a will a whole lot of money for them to go to California. So they went off to California."

Antiabduction measures may help deter kidnappings by strangers, says Dr. Lewis. But they're unlikely to prevent a mother from driving up and tooting the horn as the kids are walking home from school. There's no training in the world, he says, that will protect your children against abduction "by a loving person, particularly the other parent."

This is not very reassuring, particularly to parents who are worried that their spouse may be dangerous or sexually abusive to the kids. What Dr. Lewis suggests is to just tell your child beforehand that if such an abduction takes place, "to go with the natural parent if it feels uncomfortable to fight it. 'Then, once you're away, call me, from anywhere, and just tell me where you are.' " This seems a sensible, last-resort measure, and of course you should prepare for it by teaching your youngster how to use the phone and how to place a collect long-distance call home.

None of this, perhaps, would have saved five-year-old Sonia Montalvo, whose body was recovered from the Hudson River several months after her noncustodial father disappeared with her, but it's better than nothing.

Perhaps the only really effective deterrent to parental abduction is to work out divorce-related differences right away. Kathy Rosenthal of Children's Rights of Florida thinks the divorce laws themselves need reform so that there can be "some type of mediation between the parties to get the bitterness and angers from their married life out in the open *before* they try to decide key issues like who should get the children. I tell them to get together with a family counselor, not to mend the marriage, but to make it a good divorce. . . . When no one is a loser, the children aren't losers."

# 10

## *Stopping Physical and Sexual Abuse*

### Unwinding the Spiral of Rage

Parents don't want to hit their children. They tend to do it in moments of explosive frustration, isolation, and despair. The child's behavior at that moment may be the occasion, but it is not the cause of the parent's feelings of rage. Often there's a whole complex of problems, from financial to marital to spiritual.

For most of us, life is fraught with frustrations, and there's a tendency to take them out on our kids, especially if they've picked the wrong day to be bratty. Each of us has his own ways of controlling the urge to shout or slap. One friend, a busy, self-employed single mom, tells me that when she got frazzled and the urge to hit her ten-year-old daughter became nearly overpowering, she'd reach out and grab the child's hand. Without letting go, she'd give three little finger-taps on the girl's wrist. That was a code that stood for the three words "I love you."

And the daughter, even if she was furious and too close to hysterics to trust herself to speak, would give two little answering scratches on her mother's palm, meaning "How much?"

As answer, the mother would squeeze the girl's hand real hard, often with a funny, fierce expression to go with it. "*That* much!" was the message.

This secret, nonverbal code would often break the tension and make more reasonable discussion possible. Having secrets, then, can sometimes be a wonderful thing, if they aren't secrets from your child, but secrets *with* your child.

Try to halt the spiral of rage in yourself and in your child before emotions reach a rolling boil. Work out with your child some secret codes and strategies that only the two of you know. After all, both parent and child want to be pulled back from the brink.

Children can, in fact, be a great resource in the effort to prevent physical abuse. Often they may seem to be the problem, but the truth is that you and they have a *mutual* problem, to which you all may contribute solutions. Talk with your children about how to establish peace in the home. They have as great a stake in this as you do. Listen accurately to what they're saying and make sure they listen to you. Negotiate solutions to conflicts. Make friends with your kids. They should be your allies, not your adversaries.

If, in spite of these efforts, you find yourself in danger of losing control, or if you recognize some of the danger signs we spoke of in Chapter Three, the most important immediate step is to get yourself physically away from your child, at least for a few minutes. Even if he or she is as close as the next room, get a wall between you until you've cooled down enough to go back and discuss the problem calmly.

It is also essential to find another adult to talk with. Isolation breeds despair, and despair generates the kind of helpless anger that can lead to child abuse. A neighbor or a family member is perhaps best, but even a voice on a telephone hot line can make a crucial difference during times of crisis. Keep hot-line or friends' numbers handy by the telephone.

Also, schedule time for yourself. You're an adult with a life of your own, buried as it may often be beneath a mound of parental obligations. Have somebody you trust take over the helm for a while—even for a short while—so that you can get away and think your own thoughts.

Many divorced mothers find themselves in financial straits and may not be able to afford sitters very often; but there are usually neighbors or nearby relatives. It's important not to allow a misguided pride or shyness to keep you from getting the help you need. You might even work out, on a rotating basis, an exchange of services with the neighbors. One mother might take in several neighborhood children for an afternoon, and then the next day another mother might do the same. That way everyone would get some free time during the week.

Older people tend to be the most underestimated and underused resource that a community has. They often have more time than do younger, career-bent folks, and they may be more than happy to help. Arrange a community meeting to discuss this possibility with the senior citizens. All the parents in the community could benefit. And the children probably would, too, since old people can teach them things that many parents cannot. One of the worst aspects of our society's tendency toward age segregation is the way it deprives kids of nourishing and humanizing contacts with older people. They really do know something—something indefinable and essential—that most of us are not yet on to.

So there are usually a number of ways that we as parents can break out of our isolation and find help from those around us. And if we can't we must not hesitate to look for help from social service organizations, some of which offer counseling and other assistance.

But assuming that the children in our home are relatively safe from the tragedy of child abuse, we must also be aware of the other kids in the neighborhood. If we are a friend or relative of someone we think is abusing his child, we may be able to help by offering our patient and noncondemning friendship.

"Noncondemning" is the key, otherwise our offer of friendship will be (rightly) rejected. Suppose we live in an apartment building and a new tenant, a youngish divorcée with several children, moves in down the hall. Often as we pass her apartment we hear her shouting voice, a crashing of furniture, and long wailing cries from the children. When we see the kids, in the elevator or in the mail room, they seem sullen and uncommunicative. There are sometimes angry bruises on their faces or arms. We're concerned, and we try to be especially friendly with the mother, to get to know her and to find out what's going on; but she seems to want to keep to herself. We never see other adults going to her apartment and we worry that the woman doesn't have friends or family in the area.

Too often, concerned neighbors give up quickly after the first rebuff. But, for the children's sake, they shouldn't. It takes awhile for a mistrustful person to open up. Without being pushy, it might be possible to invite her in for a cup of coffee or offer to help her out with the kids some after-noon. If you do begin to get through to her, you could help enormously just by being there for her to turn to when the stress gets to be too much.

If you can't get through at all, and if you observe injuries on the children more than once, it may be time to call for help. You don't want to call the police or the child welfare agency too soon, but you certainly don't want to call them too late, either. Keep an eye out for the following indicators. If you see *several* of them, it may be time to act:

The child seems generally fearful, and particularly fear-ful of his parent(s).

The child shows signs of repeated injuries.

The child looks undernourished, or is given food or drink inappropriate to children.

The child isn't dressed warmly on a snowy day, or is otherwise inappropriately dressed for the weather.

A young child is confined, in crib or carriage or empty apartment, for unconscionable lengths of time.

The child acts withdrawn and cries often. Or else the child is unusually destructive and aggressive.

The child seems to take over the role of parent and tries to "mother" or otherwise protect his parent(s).

As for the parent, he or she seems very much isolated and has no adults to talk with.

The parent is distrustful of others and is unwilling to talk about his or her problems.

The parent doesn't let his or her child have normal contacts with other kids.

The parent often speaks negatively of the child, ignores the child's crying, or reacts with extreme impatience.

The parent seems to have unrealistic expectations of the child (e.g., that he should be mature beyond his years or should take care of the parent).

The parent doesn't explain the child's injuries logically or blames somebody else (or the child himself) for them.

The parent seems to have a drug or alcohol problem.

The parent admits that he or she was abused as a child or was brought up under conditions of harsh discipline.

The parent says he thinks harsh discipline is the only way to bring up kids.

The parent seems to have a mental problem—wild mood swings, for instance, and a lack of control—or he or she seems to be of borderline intelligence.

All that makes for a depressing laundry list, but it's one that you may want to refer to if you find that a neighbor (or the neighbor's child) is showing some of these characteristics.

Many times, teachers are the ones who can spot an abused child, since they see kids every day. If you're a teacher or work with children in other capacities, you should be concerned if you notice *any* of the following signs:

The child is often absent or late. Or, conversely, the child arrives too early and hangs around after classes for no apparent reason. (He may be afraid to go home.)

The child's unkempt, badly dressed for the weather, or seems in general poorly cared for.

The child more than occasionally shows up bearing bruises or welts.

The child's behavior tends to the extreme. He may be hyperactive, aggressive, disruptive, destructive. Or, conversely, he may be withdrawn, shy, passive, uncommunicative.

The child seems undernourished.

The child is often tired and falls asleep in class.

As for the parent, he or she doesn't show up for school appointments and shows little concern for the child's progress or problems.

The parent doesn't participate in any school activities and/or discourages the child from participating in them.

The parent is not known to the other parents or children.

The parent becomes aggressive or abusive when asked to discuss the child's problems in school.

The parent is observed to behave in bizarre or irrational ways, or he/she appears to be drunk.

If you observe people with some of these characteristics (derived from compilations by Dr. Vincent J. Fontana), you may well have to contact the local child welfare agency. This, in spite of one study indicating that 85 percent of the children who eventually died of parentally inflicted injuries had been referred to two or more social agencies before their final beating. Social agencies are not, in themselves, the answer. They're in dire need of streamlining, and they should be made more accountable for their frequent bureaucratic errors. But they're better than nothing.

Whatever these agencies accomplish, the key to any long-range solution to child abuse lies in the cohesiveness of the local community. As neighbors and fellow parents, we have to do what we can to maintain a grass-roots support system of social connection, a "network of kin and community," as one sociologist puts it.

If you want to help it's often possible to work under the aegis of a hospital or social agency as a lay therapist. This involves regular home visits and continuous availability to the distressed family. Parents often feel more at ease with such paraprofessionals than they would with bureaucratic officials.

Another parent-focused program is the "crisis nursery," or residential facilities for child abusers who want to get away from the stressful home environment for a cooling-off period. These refuges (what few of them exist) are often located in churches or other family-centered institutions.

A useful self-help organization is Parents Anonymous, organized by a former abusing parent to help other abusers or potential abusers. In a supportive, noncritical atmosphere, members meet weekly to tell their experiences and share their feelings. They exchange first names and telephone numbers and have a hot line for times of stress. For information on how to set up (or find) a Parents Anonymous, call 1-800-462-6406.

Sometimes police, too, can be effective in prevention efforts. In mid-1984 the New York City Police Department instituted a one-year experiment that pairs police officers with family counselors in an effort to help problem households before more violence erupts. This kind of "pro-active" (rather than merely reactive) program is being watched to see if physical abuse can in fact be prevented.

The prevention program was launched at a time when the trend is to start treating child battery as a crime rather than as a private family problem. In April 1984 the New York police commissioner instituted a new policy. He ordered that officers responding to violent family situations would no longer have to act "as mediators and social workers," but would instead make *arrests*. In that way they'd get alleged child abusers out of the house right away. Such a policy reflects a major shift in attitude. Before, the primary concern was to keep the family together. Now, it seems, the safety of the child is being put first.

Maybe this dual approach by the New York police—being at once tougher on abusers and more concerned about their plight—is a good one. In theory, at least, it certainly seems an improvement over society's usual approach to child abuse: ignoring the problem, then bandaging it in red tape and hoping it will heal itself.

## Outsmarting Molesters

The friendly stranger in the school yard may be an innocent, good-natured guy, and it's a shame that we have to view him with a degree of suspicion. But that's where our society is right now. Our overriding concern must be to protect our children from possible harm. If the stranger really is a good guy, he'll understand that.

Protecting kids from molesters is a formidable task. Many of the techniques we'd use are the same as for protecting children from kidnappers. Thus, as we suggested in Chapter 8, a child should never get in a car with a stranger, should never wander about alone, especially in deserted areas, and should be wary of such lures as the offer of affection, the use of bribery, or the request for help. The child should beware of flattery as well, and above all should understand that he must not go anywhere with a stranger without his parents' permission.

The problem is that kids aren't usually molested by

strangers. Ninety percent of the time, the child is molested by a Boy Scout leader, a school-bus driver, a friend's father, a lecherous uncle, or someone he sees almost every day. How do you protect your child against grown-ups that he knows and trusts?

• The first and most important way we can protect our child is to listen to him or her openly and attentively. If an adult is making the child uncomfortable or touching him in ways that he doesn't like, the child will find some way of hinting that all is not well. Our problem is that we tend to listen with half an ear and so may miss the hidden message. When we do decode the message, we should believe it. Kids almost never make up stories about being sexually molested.

• Teach your young child the difference between "good touch" and "bad touch." Mary Ellen Stone, director of King County Rape Relief, is one of a number of persons who go to schools to talk with kids about problems they may have with touching: good touches (like a friendly hug), bad touches (like a pinch or hit), or touches that may be uncomfortable or confusing (like having an adult put his hand on a little girl's thigh). Your child must understand that his body is his own domain and that *no one* is allowed to touch him without his permission. Let him know that he has this power over his own body.

• Reinforce this message (and help other children learn it) by arranging for your child's school or day-care center to institute safety-instruction programs and show child-protection films. One very good one is the PBS multipart show, *Child Sexual Abuse: What Your Children Should Know,* produced by WTTW in Chicago and distributed by the Indiana University Audio-Visual Center. Also, the police usually can send someone to the school to talk about safety to the kids. But try to have him meet with small groups. A lecture in front of a full auditorium, with no role-playing or other interaction, is not likely to be effective.

There are also many nonprofit groups that will visit your

child's school, often at no charge. In New York, for instance, there's the Safety and Fitness Exchange (SAFE), which offers personal safety programs, with an emphasis on the martial arts.

• Teach your young child to *tell*, if something does happen or seems close to happening. Even if the child has broken some rule (like staying up much too late watching TV with the baby-sitter), he must *tell* if the baby-sitter behaves in a sexually abusive way. Assure your child that he or she won't get in trouble for telling. Molesters often try to get children to keep a secret, "just between you and me." This mustn't be allowed to happen.

Also, with molestation by trusted adults, the abuse often happens in stages, much like a gradual seduction; if the child tells right away, he may prevent the worst from happening. And children know. They can quickly detect the difference between a simple loving hug and a sexual advance, even though they may not know how to articulate that difference.

• Let your child know that he or she has a perfect right to refuse unwanted embraces. Don't order the child to give Uncle Joe a great big kiss. Children will hug and kiss when they feel that it's natural. When it doesn't feel natural, it can be torture for them. And, of course, if Uncle Joe is inclined to sexual abuse, kids will be even more reluctant. Let your child know that it's okay to say hello or good-bye in any way he wants. He can wave, shake hands, or just stand clear across the room and say good-bye. To force a child into any grown-up's arms is to give exactly the wrong signal: that he must obey the amatory wishes of adults.

• When there *is* an unwelcome advance of some kind, be sure your child knows he has the clear option to say "No" and walk (even run) away, no matter how trusted, well loved, or close to the family the molester may be. Often, the best protection against molestation by a trusted adult is a firm, clear, loud "No!"

## A Few Words About Baby-sitters

Many thousands of young children are molested by the people we parents hire to watch over them. But even if the baby-sitter is honest and conscientious, many children are abducted from under their noses. A baby-sitter was asleep in the living room when beautiful three-year-old Ryan Burton was stolen from her crib in Breckenridge, Texas, in 1981. In mid-1984 Ryan's remains were found.

• In hiring a baby-sitter, try to get someone you already know well and have a good feeling about.

• Have a prospective baby-sitter give references from previous employers.

• Take the baby-sitter aside the first time he or she comes over and explain the house rules. Among them: fire exits, phone numbers of doctors, bedtime, and so on. But also: to let no one in the house before you come home. And equally important to make clear: "We don't have secrets in this house. If anyone tries to get our child to keep a secret or not tell his parents something, he *will* tell."

• Make sure you've trained your child to do just that. As John Conti, a professor at the University of Chicago's School of Social Services Administration, observes, "[Sexual molestation] cannot take place if it is known. Deviant acts require secrecy."

• Give your child permission to question the baby-sitter's authority. *Never* tell him (as most parents do), "Now, be sure and do what the baby-sitter tells you to." The child must be thoroughly pretrained in good-touch/bad-touch concepts, thoroughly assured that his "private zone" is indeed private, and that if anyone touches him there without his permission he can firmly say "No."

• To protect both the baby-sitter and your child, don't have the sitter tell anyone on the phone that nobody's at home. He or she should simply say that no one else can come to the phone right now, but would the caller leave a message?

• If your baby-sitter has a boyfriend who wants to visit her during her tour of duty, you should learn all you can about him too. If that is not possible, he shouldn't be allowed to visit.

# 11

# Choosing
# a Day-Care Center

The year 1984 was when America really woke up to the potential for danger in our current day-care system—or more accurately our *lack* of a system. First, there came the indictments of seven teachers at a preschool in Manhattan Beach, California. The defendants were charged with an incredible 208 counts of sexual abuse over a ten-year period. (In June 1985 a number of those counts were dropped, owing to the unwillingness of some children to testify.)

Using anatomically correct dolls, a child-sex-abuse expert named Kee MacFarlane was able to get the youngsters to express what had been happening to them. Two of the girls, independent of each other, took a piece of string to bind and gag an unclothed female doll. That's how these silenced and traumatized children were able to reveal that they themselves had been tied up when naked. Gradually children brought out detail after frightening detail; they spoke of red liquids and pink pills that made them drowsy. They spoke of threats, of guns; they spoke of rabbits, turtles, and other animals being slaughtered in their presence in order to keep them frightened into silence.

Almost as shocking, to many people, as the high number of criminal counts in the case was the presence of the seventy-seven-year-old founder of the school, Virginia Mc-

Martin, among the accused. Also indicted were her fifty-seven-year-old daughter and two McMartin grandchildren, Peggy Ann, twenty-eight, and Raymond, twenty-five.

We tend to look for child molesters among socially disaffected, psychologically bent, sexually hopped-up males on the fringes of respectable society. Matronliness and sexual molestation simply don't go together in America's myth-prone, apple-pie-on-the-windowsill view of society. And the idea of sexual perversion extending well into a woman's old age—it's just too much. If we can't trust the kindly old grandmothers in our midst, whom *can* we trust?

It's also very unsettling to realize that six of the seven indictments in the case were against women. This goes not only against our psychological stereotypes of molesters, but also against statistics. By far, most molesters are men.

In New York City, a few months later, the statistical imbalance was corrected when six male workers in a Bronx day-care center were indicted for sexually abusing scores of little children in their care. Within the week several nearby New Jersey centers were also cited for child abuse.

During this same summer, scandals hit southern Florida. A two-and-a-half-year-old boy was apparently sodomized by two janitors in a Miami Beach nursery school. The child was soon waking up his parents at night with nightmare screams of "Give me back my pants!" The two janitors were dismissed by the nursery school and questioned by the police, but no charges have been brought against the men.

Most child abuse does not, of course, take place in day-care centers. It takes place in the home. But something about the day-care scandals has really touched a nerve this past year. No doubt it has to do with the extreme youth and vulnerability of the victims. Dr. Bettye M. Caldwell, professor of child development and early education at the University of Arkansas at Little Rock, suspects that the day-care industry has been unfairly stigmatized. A *New York Times* article (September 4, 1984) quotes her as saying, "I do feel

that always lurking beneath the surface are negative feelings about day care. That is the feeling of nonworking parents about working parents. And when we have these
incidents of abuse at day-care centers, these latent negative
feelings surface."

There's also the latent or not-so-latent guilt that many
working parents feel about depositing their kids in day-care
facilities in the first place. To learn that some of these centers have been implicated in child molestation can seem an
indictment of the parents as well. The guilt and frustration
may be further exacerbated by a sense of helplessness: Yes,
we unknowingly put our children at risk, but what else
could we have done? It's not easy to find day care of any
kind these days. We had to take what we could find.

How can we make sure that the day-care center we
choose for our children is in fact safe?

The short answer is that we can't. There are, however, a
number of precautions we can take and questions we can
ask that would greatly minimize the chance that our children will be harmed.

• Make sure that the facility has an up-to-date license, if
one is required. About 90 percent of day care in this country
is underground, asserts Dr. Alfred Kahn of Columbia University. "It's not licensed, it's not regulated, and you have to
assume that a lot of it is very low quality. We have some
excellent care, and the research shows that either kids gain
or aren't hurt by day care. However, the research hasn't
gone into places that aren't licensed and aren't standard-
ized, so I would have to guess that there are a lot of terrible
things out there."

Licensing, certainly, does not guarantee good day care,
but (unless we're talking about some informal home-care
arrangement) the absence of a license needs to be ex-
plained. According to Larry Bolten of the California Department of Social Services, the number of licenses revoked
because of abuse of children increased tenfold since 1978,

to about two hundred; and most of those cases involved sexual abuse.

• Be sure that the ratio of teachers to children is high enough. One (generally ignored) set of federal guidelines recommends a ratio of one adult to three children if the children are infants. For two-year-olds the ratio is one to four. For children from age three to six, the ratio might be one adult to eight kids. Preschoolers over three years old tend to thrive in these larger groups; they're more independent and more inclined to socialize with other kids. If there are too many children per adult, as is frequently the case, effective and stimulative care is less likely to occur. In the worst places there's an impersonal, child-kennel atmosphere. State standards are often very lax in this regard, and they vary from state to state.

• Find out if there's a high rate of staff turnover. This is a problem endemic to the child-care industry, in part because of the meager salaries that staff members are paid. In the larger centers most workers receive the minimum wage. Day care in homes brings even lower wages. An estimated 87 percent of these workers make less than the minimum wage. *The New York Times* (September 2, 1984) quotes San Francisco public opinion analyst Mervin D. Field as saying, "Women are going pell-mell into the labor force, and they've been desperate to get someone to take care of their kids. There's been such a demand that some of these day-care centers are no more than warehouses operated by untrained people who are just a notch above street people."

Certainly this description does not apply to the many thousands of dedicated child-care workers in this country, but the disgracefully low pay scale makes it impossible to attract a great many highly trained people. And those it does manage to hire tend to leave after a year or two in search of a livable wage. This is not good for children. They tend to do best when they're cared for by the same people consistently.

• Find out if the staff is qualified. We just spoke about why much of the staff may not be. And again, requirements vary widely from state to state. In New York state if a center has more than forty-five children, there must be at least one staff member with two years' teaching experience and a state certificate (or the equivalent) in early childhood education. In New Jersey a head teacher must have a bachelor's degree, two years' experience, and state certification. An assistant teacher must have the equivalent of two years of college with at least fifteen credits in early childhood education, plus one year of experience. A teacher's aide must have a high school diploma or have children enrolled at the center. In Connecticut a teacher or assistant must be at least eighteen and have a high school diploma. Aides must be at least sixteen and need not meet any educational requirements. Not very reassuring, is it? The staff/child ratio isn't so terrific in Connecticut, either: one adult for every ten kids, regardless of the child's age.

In most states the requirements for the head teacher are adequate to assure at least some knowledgeability. The teacher's aides, however, need know almost nothing at all; and it is they who are most frequently in contact with the children. Ten million working mothers have children under five years old, and their numbers keep increasing. Yet, according to the National Association of Social Workers, only about *one fourth* of all day-care employees have been professionally trained to work with children.

• Find out if the center does criminal background checks on its staff. Many states have no such requirement, and state agencies don't have the money, the manpower, or in some cases the willpower to regulate the day-care industry rigorously. Texas is one state that requires a check for criminal background among new employees, but the checking may sometimes be superficial, allowing offenders to slip through. New York City has not had a policy of checking for criminal background, but in the wake of the sex-abuse scandals in several Bronx day-care centers it has instituted a policy of fingerprinting employees and prospective employees. In New York state, names of prospective employees are now being checked against the state's Central Register for Child Abuse. Of course, many child abusers (probably most) are not in the Central Register. But it's a start.

Oddly enough, New Jersey does not check employees for criminal records, but it requires prospective employees to disclose any arrests or convictions. As if a man with a string of child-molestation convictions is going to volunteer that information. In fact, that man is probably applying for a day-care job to be near his intended prey. When the notorious bank robber, Willie Sutton, was asked why he robbed banks, he said, "Because that's where the money is." Child molesters may be drawn to day-care work because that's where the children are.

If there is no state requirement to make criminal background checks, at least find out as much as you can about the people your children will be spending their days with. That means not just the teachers, but also the aides, cooks, and other employees. Ask about them. Talk to them. Get a feel for the kind of people they are.

• Find out how often the facility is inspected and when the last inspection was. Your child's safety is not guaranteed simply because the staff is cheerful and helpful and molester-free. There are also building codes, safety regulations, and a host of other questions to consider. A Texas day-care licenser notes that in that state there's been a 120 percent increase in the number of facilities since 1977; but in that same period there's been a 60 percent decrease in the number of inspectors. So Texas day-care centers have gone from about four inspections per year in 1977 to one every six to nine months in 1984. That's a lot better than in California, where facilities may be inspected once every three years, unless a specific complaint has been received about unsafe conditions.

• Give the place an informal inspection yourself. Are there secure screens or bars on windows above the first floor? Are there clearly marked and unobstructed fire exits? Is the place clean? Does the kitchen seem sanitary? How nutritious are the meals that are served there? Is there adequate equipment, including appropriate toys for your child's age group? Is there enough room for children to play? Has the place been "childproofed" so that youngsters will not hit themselves against sharp edges or cut themselves with unsafe, easily splintered toys? Finally, what is the administration's attitude toward your poking around and asking all these questions? If they seem hostile or defensive, that could mean they have something to hide.

• Look closely at the curriculum they offer your child. Ralph Nader has described some day-care setups as "children's warehouses." In many mediocre facilities the quality of attention to the children is indifferent and the educational planning inferior. There are places where there seems no plan at all, where children spend an aimless, meaningless, uninspired, and poorly supervised day, sometimes in front of a television set.

• Try to find the time to spend at least one day in the center yourself. It's an enlightening experience and will tell you more about the quality of care your child is receiving than all the assurances in the world from day-care operators. The investment of that day may also be important in less tangible ways. Parents have a tendency to see their children as components in the parents' own lives. A day spent in a child-care facility reverses that perspective and makes one realize—often with the force of a revelation—that children have their own day to get through. It's a secret glimpse into their real nine-to-five world and the life they lead apart from their family. So *this* is what Jesse (or Monica, or Perry) does all day! These are the people he spends much of his waking life with. These are the things he does. This is the way he's talked to. This is what he's really up against.

Often the revelation is mostly pleasant—the child really does seem to be happily playing and learning; and, yes, he is getting adequate nap time and decent if unexciting food. (The food will *not* be exciting.) On the other hand, if the feeling of the place is not happy, not caring, and if the children seem bored or worse, that, too, will become quickly evident. Put it this way: if your one day in their day-care-center world strikes you as intolerable and something you would never want to repeat, it probably is for them too. Maybe you should look for a better facility.

• Be sure there's good communication between you and those running the center. This means they must call you if anything unusual comes up. If the child has to be released early, for instance, you should be informed so that he isn't left waiting on the street for you to come. If you have to be a little bit late, arrange that the child can stay in the center that extra time (provided, of course, there are some responsible adults still there). In any case be sure to get to know other parents; if the center can't keep your child on those occasional days when you're late, work something out with the parents of one of your child's day-care chums. The more people you know and regularly communicate with at the center, the broader your child's safety net. However, be absolutely sure that the day-care center does not release your child to anyone but you unless they have your specific permission to do so.

• Inquire about health precautions. Day-care centers, like schools, are often breeding grounds for contagious diseases. What is the center's medical setup and how qualified are those who administer it? What is the policy if an obviously sick child shows up at the center in the morning? What if your own child gets sick while there? Will the center call you at work and tell you? Does the staff take yearly medical checkups and tuberculosis tests? Do teachers encourage good health and hygiene habits in the kids? Are the bathrooms sanitary and the rooms adequately ventilated?

• Do the people taking care of your child seem to have any spark of imagination? This is a tough one, because *nobody* is good enough to take care of a parent's miraculous and absolutely unique child. But on the other hand, there are a lot of dullards and sluggards in the day-care industry, and it's a shame to waste your child's time with them if there's some way of getting a bright and lively teacher who will teach the child new physical skills, will stimulate him to use his imagination, will encourage verbal and creative expression, will let the child make some choices for himself and take as much responsibility as he can handle.

It would be nice if the teacher were not rigid and hidebound, if he or she provided a clear routine and understandable rules but was also able to vary the activities and come up with challenging new projects. And how about group trips to nearby parks, museums, baseball fields? This is, after all, your child's life. It's essential to find a child-care program that manages to avoid the extremes of chaos and sloppy discipline on the one hand and grim regimentation on the other.

• Become involved and involve other parents. This may at first seem unreasonable, since one has sought the services of a day-care center in the first place because there simply wasn't time to be taking care of children in the middle of the day. But day care has been given a low priority and reduced public funding in recent years and it needs all the help it can get. Naturally, parents should be wary of child-care centers that don't encourage parental involvement, don't allow unannounced visits, or won't give out the names and phone numbers of other parents who have children enrolled there. Any center that has nothing to hide will welcome parental involvement and actively seek it out.

And we all have an occasional day or half-day off from work. Parents are a virtually untapped reservoir of talents and special expertise. If you can do something, if you're an artist, dancer, musician, come in sometime and spend an

afternoon sharing that ability with the kids. If you're a policeman or computer expert or jeweler or doctor, arrange to
come in and tell the kids about what you do. Or just volunteer some day to help chaperone the next bus trip to a state
park. Extra eyes and ears and helping hands are always
needed on such excursions.

In short, if your day-care center is basically adequate but
is not quite all you would want it to be, help to make it
better. Day care in this country should not simply be
viewed as a fully formed, preexistent service of which we
have only to avail ourselves; it is, rather, a gradually developing solution to some of the problems parents are faced
with these days. It is only a partial solution, tentatively
arrived at, and should not be left solely in the hands of
administrators or governmental regulators.

There are now a number of commercial day-care chains
such as Kinder-Care, La Petite Academies, and Children's
World, Inc., and some of these have hundreds of "outlets."
Clearly, the patchwork approach of the past is inadequate
to the burgeoning day-care needs of the future, but one gets
an uneasy feeling from these slick new chains as well. They
seem the McDonald's, Burger King, and Wendy's of day
care. If we entrust our children to them will they come out
prepackaged adultlets, containing the approved proportion
of socialization, sanitized thought, and obedience?

The truth is, if we want our children to have the best day
care possible, we're going to have to fight for it. We may
have to struggle to improve the disorganized and under-
funded mom-and-pop day-care centers, and we may have
to raise a stink to get the attention of the new corporate
child-care franchisers. Whatever is necessary, we will have
to do it. Child care is not something taken out of our hands
once and for all during the hours we are at our jobs. It needs
constant fixing and tinkering and attention. It is a nuisance,
like much of daily life. But we must never make the mistake
of thinking that anyone, whether child-care "expert" or

child psychiatrist, really knows what is best for our children.

Certainly the government hasn't shown much noticeable wisdom or compassion in its approach to the day-care phenomenon. One recalls that after President Nixon vetoed the Child Development Act in 1972 conservatives cheered, thinking that they were sending mothers everywhere the message that they should get back in the home where they belonged. Since 1981 the Reagan administration seems to have been trying to send mothers the same message. It cut federal subsidies for child care, effectively denying that service to many children of poor parents. This at a time when day care costs have risen to an average $5,000 per child annually. An article in *Newsweek* (September 10, 1984) gives an estimate that in the state of California a single working mother with a child under the age of two must spend 49 percent of her income on child care. A two-parent family earning $24,000 per year will spend 26 percent of its gross income on day care for two small children.

That's if they can find any day care at all. There are in this country perhaps as many as five million kids under the age of ten who have nobody to look after them during the afternoon. Waiting lists for day-care centers and after-school centers are sometimes years long. A child could "age out" of the day-care system before he can get into it.

It is the "seller's market" in day care that creates many of the dangers we read about. Single parents who are trying to stay off welfare, as well as two-parent families where both partners work, are finding themselves in a bind. They might like to take all the sage suggestions in this chapter—judging and weighing the merits of various day-care centers—but they may find themselves so desperate for *any* day-care help at all that they don't inquire too closely about the fine points of a given facility. It could be argued that, by cutting funds for child care in this country, our government is creating a climate that encourages abuses in the industry. Even shoddy day-care operations will find plenty of little clients clamoring to get in. Yes, even facilities with untrained, unscreened staff.

To get child molesters out of our day-care system it will take more than background checks and other Band-Aid measures. It will take a total commitment to the improvement of the whole system. That means, first of all, a lot more money from the federal government so that the pay scale for staff can be raised to the human level without impoverishing parents who want day care for their kids. It means, on the most basic level, a governmental acknowledgment that society is different from the way it was fifty or even twenty years ago, and that day care is a fact of life, to be dealt with intelligently and compassionately, and to be made as safe as it can possibly be.

## IF YOU CAN'T BE AT HOME (AND YOUR CHILD IS)

Eventually your child will outgrow the day-care center. Many parents of young children find themselves in a real bind when the kids start grade school, especially if both parents have to work. The child may get home at 2:00 or 3:00, the mother and father at 6:00 or later. The term "latchkey kids" has been used to designate these children, but it has a negative connotation, as if it were the parents' fault that they can't be there. The Center for Early Adolescence in North Carolina prefers the term "the 3-to-6-P.M. issue."

There are a couple of ways to deal with this issue. One is to look into services and after-school programs that are available in your local school, library, Boy Scout troop, and numerous other organizations. If such services don't exist, parents might contact these places, and their PTA, and try getting them started. In the meantime, neighbors could be mobilized to cooperate in looking after kids. It's surprising how many alternatives you may discover to leaving the kids alone in the house during those afternoon hours.

If you have no choice but to leave them by themselves, the National Crime Prevention Council in Washington, D. C., has a few suggestions:

1. Have your child check in with you by phone after he arrives home. The child should know your work number and have it on his person (as well as taped up by the phone).

2. Another number to have ready by the phone is a "warm line." If you aren't reachable and your child is lonely, he can call one of these special lines and talk to a friendly, informed grown-up. To find out how to establish a warm line in your community, contact Phone Friend, Inc., American Association of University Women, State College Branch, P.O. Box 735, State College, PA 16804. They'll be glad to send you a kit and information.

3. Work out an arrangement with a trusted neighbor or with a prearranged "safe house" where your child knows he can go if he's feeling scared or upset.

4. Teach your child how to get out of the house quickly, in case of fire or other dangers.

5. Teach him how to answer the phone. The child mustn't say that nobody's at home but "Mommy can't come to the phone now. Can I take a message?"

6. When your child's alone in the house it's best for him *not* to answer the door.

7. Teach him how to work the locks and bolts on all doors and windows. Your child should keep these locked when he's alone in the house.

8. If he comes home and finds the door ajar or a window broken, your child should *not* go in. Have him go straight to a trusted neighbor's house and call you from there.

9. Teach your child how to use both push-button and

dial phones, as well as how to dial long-distance. Lists of important numbers should be kept by the telephone at all times.

10. Be sure your child knows that he must not go into other homes without your permission.

11. Be sure he understands that if anything happens to him, or if anyone tells him to keep a secret from you, he is to tell you about it at once.

12. Talk with your child frequently about what his concerns and worries are when he's alone. Work out with him what his responsibilities are. Your child must know the rules about pets, TV, homework, and must understand the limits of his freedom.

13. If you're not going to be home at the usual time be sure to let your child know this. He or she worries just as much as you do.

## PART THREE

# Strategies for Protecting Teenagers

# 12

## *Protecting Your Teenage Driver*

If your teenagers drive, that means you trust them. You've also tacitly agreed to let them take certain risks. Since they aren't under your direct control, it doesn't make much sense to issue edicts about what they shall and shall not do when they're behind the wheel and you're sitting at home. Some parents attempt to maintain control by threatening a child with ifs: "If I find you've been drinking while driving, I'll take away your driving privileges for a month."

This may, in fact, work—or appear to work. There are various styles of child-rearing, and it's not the mission of this book to pronounce one method correct and another incorrect. But it does seem that you can't trust and distrust at the same time, any more than you can simultaneously go forward and in reverse. The fact is, when you turned over the keys, you turned over the power. Your position is not that of the child's owner. At best you are his consultant. As Dr. Thomas Gordon notes in *P.E.T.—Parent Effectiveness Training,* consultants can be fired. "Today's youth," he writes, "are discharging their parents—informing them that their services are no longer desired—because few parents are effective consultants to their kids. They lecture, cajole, threaten, warn, persuade, implore, preach, moralize, and shame their kids, all in an effort to force them to do what they feel is right. . . . As consultants, most parents' attitude is that *their clients must buy;* if the clients don't, they feel they have failed. . . . No wonder that in most families kids are desperately saying to their parents, 'Get off my back,' 'Stop hassling me,' 'I know what you think, you don't need to keep telling me every day,' 'Stop lecturing me,' 'Too much,' 'Good-bye.' "

At this point a kid with a car may just drive off into the sunset. A kid without a car may stick out his thumb and start hitching. Another runaway for the police blotter.

To really protect one's child it's essential to establish a relationship of trust and openness. Most parents, from everything one reads, don't. Share your concerns about your child's safety, and make him or her a participant in solving the problem of working out a set of safety guidelines that apply to cars. After all, kids want to live. They have a stake in safety. And if they come up with some of the ideas themselves, they're likely to abide by them. Whatever arrangements you and your children work out, they must make sense to everyone involved. They must, to a considerable extent, *come from* the kids who are going to be behind the wheel. Therefore the ideas that follow are not "rules"; they're simply starting points for a family's own discussions of the subject.

1. "Don't think it can't happen to you." So says Richard Ruffino, a leading missing-children expert. There's a tendency for teenagers to feel invulnerable. Beginning to sense their own power, they may not realize that there are limits to that power. If a teen's car breaks down and someone stops to help, most likely that person's just being a good neighbor; but talk to your teenager about keeping alert to the possibility—however distant—that the helpful stranger may have ulterior motives.

In fact, that's the way Henry Lee Lucas, the self-professed mass murderer, says he used to operate. As he told newswoman Sylvia Chase in an interview for ABC's "20/20," he'd be on the lookout for young women with car trouble on the side of the road. Said Lucas, in his folksiest drawl, "I'll come up to ya and check yer car out. See if I can start it for ya. All the time I'll be thinkin', I'm not goin' to start this car, you know. If it'll start, I won't start it. I'm liable to say, 'Yer car is ruint fer good, you know, as far as the engine.' And I'll say, 'I know where's a telephone right up the road here. I'll take you up there. . . .' And by the time you realize that you done passed that telephone, it's too late."

An unknown number of serial (or recreational) murderers are out there roaming our nation's highways looking for prey. As Richard Ruffino unceremoniously sums up, "There are a lot of nice people wanting to help. But there's also a lot of crap out there."

2.  Be careful when helping other people out. Teens tend to be generous and unsuspecting people. If they see somebody whose car has had a breakdown, they may instinctively want to help. Decide with them what they might do in various hypothetical situations. Urge them to keep their eyes open and not to hesitate to roar right off if anything looks or feels suspicious. They must learn to trust their instincts, which often provide warnings before the brain can come up with corroborating evidence. There's a difference, says Dick Ruffino, "between being fearful and being cautious." Err on the side of caution.

3.  Talk with your kids about hitchhiking. There is no such thing as safe hitchhiking, and you and your children may mutually agree that they won't hitchhike themselves and won't pick up hitchhikers. That's obviously the safest course of action.

But if they're going to hitch anyway (and in some situations it's the only way to get around), talk to them about things to keep in mind. First, they should try to hitch with somebody else. The buddy system is often very helpful since would-be molesters, robbers, or killers will be wary of a double threat. This system is particularly important for long-distance hitching. Most often it's the boys who hitch for long distances, girls who hitch across town. Both are at risk, and both would be better off with traveling companions. Certainly, the most at risk would be a runaway of either sex, out in the middle of the desert or some other nowhere, hitching by himself or herself, with no money and no destination. This happens more often than one likes to think.

If you're hitching by yourself and the man who picks you up makes you nervous or starts making a sexual advance, don't be nice and polite, just get the hell out. Obviously, if you're going sixty miles an hour you can't do that; but there are likely to be red lights somewhere along the way, or places where it's at least necessary for him to slow down a bit. If the car's going only fifteen miles an hour or so, you might just take a chance on a bruised knee by hopping out.

Often a sexual advance can be stopped by a firm, loud "No!" and a "Let me out here, please." Each situation must be judged separately. But whatever your judgment, be *decisive.*

Don't immediately tell the driver your ultimate destination. When you first get in and he asks where you're headed, just say, "Up the road a ways." That way, if something about his behavior starts making you nervous, you can say, "Oh, here it is, right up here. This'll be fine. Thanks. 'Bye."

If he doesn't stop then, you know you're in trouble. If he pulls out a gun, you know you should never have decided to try hitchhiking by yourself in the first place. Most such people, unless they're simply psycho, will want you for sex or for whatever money you might be carrying. Again, assess the particular situation you're in. General rules won't help you. Be clear-headed, look him in the eye, try to reason with him. Sometimes that works, sometimes not. If he's merely in economic difficulties, get him talking about his problem and try to make friendly, helpful suggestions. If he starts considering you a confidante, he's less likely to become violent with you.

Or you may want to appear to submit. This carries its own dangers, but it's an option to consider. If he pulls a gun and says he's going to rape you, it may be possible to diminish the immediate danger by saying something like, "Hey, you don't have to pull out a gun. Maybe I want to have sex too."

"Be as conning and as cunning as they are," advises Dick Ruffino, and meanwhile get the driver to slow the car down a bit so that you can jump out. One woman, when she found that the driver wasn't about to slow down, nimbly reached over and switched off the ignition. While the car lurched and its gears ground, she was able to get out the door and roll into the grass along the shoulder of the road. But obviously such a maneuver is full of risks. She just figured it was *less* of a risk than staying in a speeding car with a man with a gun in his hand and rape on his mind.

4. Drinking and driving. This is an easy one. Don't. Some teens, though acknowledging that booze can blur their minds and slow their reaction time, are under the misapprehension that marijuana doesn't have the same effect. In fact, it can be even worse. To try driving while you're having a rush is like picking your way through a mine field by the stuttering illumination of a strobe light.

But what do you do if you've been to a party with your friends, gotten drunk or stoned, and need a way to get home? Sometimes, kids work out a deal among themselves that one or more of them will stay absolutely straight and drive the "wrecked" kids home. Or they'll work out that everybody who's too stoned to drive will crash on the living-room sofa for the night.

Then again, there are enlightened families who've agreed long beforehand that, if for any reason the kid cannot safely drive himself home, he will call home—any hour of the night or day—and somebody will come and pick him up. The deal is *no questions, no recriminations.*

5. Parking-lot assaults. Many a woman has been grabbed while trying to get into her car in a deserted parking lot late at night. If the man just wants to rob you the conventional wisdom is to give him your money without panicking or getting hysterical. But if the man wants more than that, if he wants, for instance, to get you into a car with him, conventional wisdom won't get you anywhere. It's an extremely dangerous situation, no matter what you do. So many women are forced at gunpoint into a car, only to be found dead in a nearby woods two weeks later, that it might just be worth it to put up a fight right there in the parking lot. A young woman must use everything she's got, which means screaming, kicking, scratching, punching. Nothing good is going to come of getting into a car with that man. The risk is that he'll shoot her right where she stands. The likelihood is that a much more gruesome fate awaits her if she goes with him.

Teens should try *not* to be in a deserted parking lot alone late at night in the first place. They should make a real habit of using a buddy system.

6. Driving off to college. Often, a young man or woman of eighteen or so will load up the car, wave good-bye, and head off across the country to a distant college or university. The parents, of course, are very worried until they hear that their child is safe in the dorm, although that might be three days later. It's important for teens to keep in phone contact with home during any long trip. They should call every twelve to sixteen hours and let their parents know their current location. In the unlikely but not-unheard-of event that the child disappears somewhere along the way, the parents (and the police) will at least have something to go on.

"Oh, don't worry about me, Mom. I can take care of myself." What teenager has not, with weary voice, patronized a parent in this way? And sure, they know better than to take candy from strangers, the sorts of lures little kids might be tempted by. But what about other lures? What about the earnest-looking man with three cameras dangling from his neck who approaches a young coed and says she has a special look and he'd like to take some shots of her? Maybe he can get her into *Cosmopolitan* or *Mademoiselle*. He gives her his legitimate-looking card. If she seems unconvinced, he might say, fine, there are lots of other young women who'd like to be in national magazines. Of course, she wouldn't fall for such a line, would she?

Or the guy who comes up to her (or him) and says he's doing a play, or making a movie, and "You've got the right look for one of the parts." Nobody would fall for that, right?

What about a more ordinary lure—a job? It's in a nearby city, and the pay is great. In our time of high teenage unemployment, jobs are a very tough lure to ignore. Multiple-murderer John Wayne Gacy was in the construction business, and he'd lure teenage boys to his place with promises of high-paying jobs, as high as nine dollars an hour, and this was some years ago. That's pretty good. Later, thirty-three corpses of young men were found buried beneath his house.

Beware of job offers, says Dick Ruffino, particularly high-paying or glamor jobs. It's probably a con. And beware of overfriendly people generally. Friendship is the most potent lure of all among affection-hungry adolescents. There are, of course, many genuinely affable and ingratiating people who have no evil designs whatever on youngsters. But unprefaced and excessive friendliness, an overfamiliar approach with no history of friendship to justify it, these should all arouse a youngster's suspicions.

When you add wheels to all these dangers, you increase the geographical potential for harm. The phony job offer, the acting interview, and the modeling assignment could be in a distant city, far from parental protection. Our teenagers, as they grow toward full maturity, must learn to protect themselves. We can help by being there for them—not against them—and by sitting down and working out a mutually agreeable set of safety strategies for them to use when they're out there on the highways alone.

# 13

# Preventing Date Rape

As adolescents embark on dating, they enter upon an un-known and more-than-slightly-scary behavioral region. Traditionally, boys are supposed to take the initiative, ask the girl out, try for the kiss at the door, and maybe even "cop a feel." The whole setup has built-in problems. Boys get the message from TV soap operas, James Bond movies, and locker-room talk that they're supposed to be aggressive, while girls are supposed to be passively resistant and then gradually acquiescent. Kids get the idea that sex is the best way to get close to somebody. It's the intimacy of first resort, instead of a natural evolution of a relationship based on an increasing affection and respect. It's also often confused, in some male minds, with a competitive sport—hence the tendency to talk about "scoring" with a girl. If you haven't scored you can't win.

Adolescent boys who are trying to cover their insecurities with a macho façade may start treating their female counterparts with something less than respect. If their fear is spiked with hostility they may try to force a date to go "further" than she wants to go. If they manage to convince themselves that her increasingly insistent "No!" is really "Yes!" in disguise, they may even proceed to rape.

Young women, when they think about rape, may imagine some scruffy stranger lurking in an alley and probably carrying a knife or gun. As Billie Jo Flerchinger of King County Rape Relief (Renton, Washington) pointed out in a recent PBS TV series on sexual abuse, less than 5 percent of rapists use a weapon. And the number one place of rape is not a back alley but inside the home. (The number two rape locale is the car, often in the course of a "hot date.") Ninety-nine percent of rapists are males, and they're usually young, between ages eighteen and thirty-five. Their abusive behavior tends to be evident while they're still in their teens. They are inherently angry people, often angry at (and fearful of) women; they've been (or felt) frequently rejected in their quest for approval and love and have low self-esteem. They want to humiliate their victim, the way they feel that they themselves have been humiliated in the past. Degrading a woman makes them feel temporarily powerful.

None of this has much to do with the sexual urge, but a lot to do with hostility. With "date rape" the sexual component is usually greater than with rape in general, since it tends to occur during a sexual encounter, such as petting or kissing. It can be a shortcut to gratification, without having to bother with all that mushy relationship stuff (which in fact is much scarier and more difficult to deal with than any purely sexual encounter).

Sixty percent of teen victims know their assailants. Nearly all assaults occur when the girl is alone with the guy, maybe after they've come home from a party or a movie. The young man may be misinformed about his prerogatives, imagining that if he's spent money on the girl it's okay to insist on having sex with her. He may also come out with such falsities as "If you care about me you'll go to bed with me"; or "Everyone does it"; or "I love you"; or "Don't be a baby."

A girl who's been raped by a boy she's been out with is likely to feel humiliated and afraid. Those are appropriate emotions to feel, since she *has* been degraded and endangered. But girls also tend to feel ashamed of themselves, as if it's their own fault for getting into the situation in the first place. Feeling guilty, she will usually not tell her parents and may not tell anyone at all. This reaction only compounds the injury, because victims need to talk things out, to work their way through the thickets of conflicting emotions. They should understand, as Ms. Flerchinger emphasizes in the PBS show, that "the responsibility for the rape lies 100 percent with the offender, no matter what the situation."

The tendency not to report an assault often stems not only from the victim's feelings of guilt but also from her fear that her friends will look at her differently afterward, either as a fragile and damaged vase to be handled with kid gloves or else as a tramp. But a victim's silence endangers other young women. Rapists are seldom permanently satisfied with a single rape; theirs is a compulsion that tends to recur. It's better for everybody if such a person's tendencies are revealed at once.

There are certain things one can do to minimize the chance of date rape (also called acquaintance rape).

1. Girls should know something of the background of the guys they go out with. If a young man has a history of manhandling women, he should obviously be avoided. Girls should communicate with one another about potentially dangerous characters in their midst. A high school or college is often a tight little society where "the word" can get around pretty quickly.

2. A young woman should try to take control of the dating situation early in the evening by communicating clearly her mood. Ambiguous responses to an advance can be interpreted as permission to continue. As Ms. Flerchinger remarks, "ESP doesn't work." A girl should be clear about her own sexual limits in a given situation and be definite about communicating those limits.

3. A girl should be alert for danger signals. She'll avoid

guys who act as though they know her more intimately than they really do. Some macho guys move right into another person's psychological space. They may push people around to get their way. They may not listen to what a woman is saying. Such young men are very dangerous.

4. If an assault is imminent, it is important to be direct and assertive, to stand up tall and look the guy in the eye. It's not the time to hint around.

5. If an assault is begun, many women tend to freeze with fear. Fear keeps them from thinking and acting. It's essential to get *angry*. That makes the blood and adrenaline flow; it makes the mind work fast; it gives one the force to fight.

6. The point, in dealing with an assault, is not to get the man down and out, but rather to seize the first opportunity to get away. This can mean breaking away and running. It can also mean creating a hell of a scene that will draw the attention of others to what is happening. We all have certain built-in protective skills: we can run, kick, yell. But whatever is done must be done decisively, and it must be done *early on.*

7. Since no two assaults are exactly alike, there are times when none of the above ideas will work. If there's no one around for miles and the guy has a knife, it might be the best thing to let the rape happen. That's okay too. It's not a girl's fault if she's raped. And in certain situations, giving in to it may save her life.

# 14

# *Keeping Teens from Running Away*

Most missing children are runaways. Over a million a year. And most runaway kids are teenagers. According to Kenneth Lanning, a special agent with the FBI, the youngsters at greatest risk are those between ages thirteen and twenty-three. "All the focus," he says, "is on little children who've been abducted, whereas the *big* problem is adolescent kids who leave home under a variety of circumstances."

Missing-children expert Richard Ruffino agrees that older kids are more likely to meet with harm than younger ones. "They're caring people and very vulnerable," he says. They're out from under the parental wing, at least to a degree, and they're taking a lot more risks than little kids do.

The greatest risk they can take is to run away from home. Most of those who pack up their duffle bags and hit the road are not doing it with a positive sense of adventure but because they can't communicate in any satisfactory way with their parents. The cause of this block in communication may sometimes rest with the teen himself, who may not be trying hard enough to understand his parents. But just as often, without meaning to, it's the parents who drive their child away.

An extreme example, reported in the Los Angeles *Times* (July 22, 1984), may illustrate a common problem, usually found in a much milder form:

He was the fastest 10-year-old freestyler in the nation and he kept getting better. At 12, he set a national record for his age. He was almost 6 feet tall, powerfully built, and had great flexibility and a natural feel for the water. His parents assumed he would be an Olympic champion.

But he stopped growing at 13 and his improvement slowed. He hit a plateau at 14, and could not drop his times. At 15 he began swimming slower.

His parents were furious. For nine years they had devoted their lives to swimming and they expected their son to win. They berated him constantly after meets and occasionally struck him after a poor swim.

He grew to hate swimming, but was afraid to tell his parents he wanted to quit. After years of spending up to five hours a day in the water pushing himself to exhaustion, years of frustration, years of listening to his parents tell him he was a failure, he attempted suicide by slashing his wrists.

"Both parents were very overweight, nonathletic, and they were able to prove something, get some self-worth through their son's swimming," said a Southern California swim coach who coached the boy for several years. "When he swam slowly, they felt like failures."

Parents who don't want their children to run away (or kill themselves) should keep a careful watch on their own attitudes and expectations regarding them. Do we insist that our son become a doctor or that our daughter get straight A's because we once wanted to be a doctor and we never did well academically?

Other parents have trouble dealing with their child's increasing independence. They don't want him taking the risks that adolescents want to take. Youth is the time to take risks, time to tramp around Europe if the kid can get up the airfare, time to experiment in all sorts of ways. Parents who try to protect their child in oppressively strict ways when he is well along the road to becoming an adult are likely to have a rebel on their hands. Perhaps even a runaway. And then they can't protect him at all.

Even if parents don't try to clip their adolescent's wings, and even if they don't try to turn him into a surrogate success for themselves, they very often talk to him or her in ways that they would never talk to other adults. It's all too common for parents to condescend to their child, insult him, impugn his motives, all in the name of teaching him how to behave.

Then there's the danger of being too lax. Parents who offer no guidance and set no limits and take no apparent interest in their child's development are very likely to have a child who feels unloved. In some families, financial pressures, marital discord, and other frequent crises make it possible that one child will be neglected and largely ignored —even if the parents really do love that child a great deal. Love has to be demonstrated, time has to be taken, attention paid. A child who feels superfluous and unloved may one day quietly gather his things and leave. That act is often a cry for attention.

As parents we worry that our teenager may fall in with a bad crowd. And we have cause to worry if this peer group is known for making trouble, using heavy drugs, or taking egregious risks. Peer pressure is particularly strong during the teen years, and even a good kid can be swept along with others who are into dubious activities.

At the same time *some* company is usually better than no company, even if you don't entirely approve of the company your child keeps. Rapists, abductors, and con artists of all stripes generally pick off the strays. The lonely, dejected teen wandering aimlessly around a shopping mall, or the runaway girl in a bus station looking confused about her destination, is a very vulnerable young person. Teenagers should be encouraged to have friends and to stay in groups when they're out in the street—no matter how aggravating gaggles of ragtag teens can seem to the rest of us.

Many times, teenagers run away from home after a hurtful argument with their parents. Often it centers around something the child is doing that his parents don't want him to be doing. Dr. Thomas Gordon, in his useful book *P.E.T. —Parent Effectiveness Training,* suggests that many fights can be avoided if parents and kids work out what kinds of actions affect the parents, which affect only the kids, and which affect both and therefore need to be negotiated. The son's hair length may upset the parent, but it doesn't directly affect him and therefore, really, it's none of his business. The sixteen-year-old daughter may stay up much too late, by the parent's reckoning, watching TV or reading Harlequin romances, but that, again, does not hurt the parent. "If parents would limit their attempts to modify behavior to what interferes with the parents' needs, there would be far less rebellion," says Dr. Gordon, "and fewer parent-child relationships that go sour."

A kid who refuses to do his share of the housework, or who sits talking on the phone for hours at a time when the parents would like to make some calls of their own, *is* interfering with his parents' needs, and everyone needs to get together and talk about this.

When children are very young, parents often "lay down the law," and since most of the power is on the parents' side, that *seems* to work—though in fact it sows the seeds of later rebellion. Adolescence is when that rebellion tends to break forth. The power in the family is more equally balanced then; a parent's threats hold little terror. One way to avoid bitter fights with teenage kids is not to invoke the question of power in the first place. This requires imagination and patience, and it may not work if the patterns of the past are too deeply ingrained, or if the teenager has already written his parents off as Archie Bunker–type emotional dinosaurs. Both sides have to come to the bargaining table willing to negotiate.

Take the teenager who monopolizes the family's one telephone, for instance. This is a problem for the parents; the parents "own" the problem, and a solution must be found that solves it to the parents' satisfaction. Maybe a second phone could be installed in the teenager's room. If that's economically difficult, perhaps the teen could pay the monthly bill himself. Paying it would be *his* problem, but in return he could talk on the phone all night long if he wanted. With this sort of arrangement, the parents aren't wielding tyrannical power over the child, and the child is not treating his parents like doormats.

Dr. Gordon urges parents to engage in "active listening" when their youngsters are telling them something. Like the rest of us, kids tend to "encode" their meaning, throwing out vague indirect signals that it is the listener's job to "decode" correctly. To take a simple example, when a child asks his mother "Is dinner ready?" she may *think* that his message is "I want to go out and meet my friends and I want to get this dinner business over quickly." If that is indeed his message, then Mom has decoded it correctly, and she may feel justified in responding with annoyance: "Your friends will just have to wait. I've been cooking for hours and I don't want you rushing through dinner like you usually do!"

But what if his message is simply "I'm hungry"? What's the kid going to think of his mother's outburst? He's likely to say, "Mom, you're weird," and walk out of the house and skip dinner altogether.

In active listening, the parent will simply "play back" the message that he's received, so that the child can confirm it as correct or deny it.

CHILD: Is dinner ready yet?
MOTHER: You want to eat soon?

CHILD: Yeah, I'm really starving!

MOTHER: You're really hungry? You don't just want to get it over with so you can go out and see your friends?

CHILD: Nah, they're not even around today. I just didn't get much to eat for lunch.

MOTHER: Well, we're going to eat soon, but if you really can't wait, why don't you take a cookie?

Needless arguments start with simple misunderstandings and escalate to complicated misunderstandings. All this can usually be avoided if both parent and child try to put aside their preset negative attitudes and approach their conversation with an open mind, "actively" listening to be sure they understand what's really being said. If it turns out that there is a conflict between the child's needs or desires and those of the parent, there are ways of *negotiating* a compromise acceptable to both parties without resorting to power plays.

But this approach requires open minds as well as open ears, and it entails a certain element of risk. Says Dr. Gordon, "People actually become changed by what they *really understand*. To be 'open to the experience' of another invites the possibility of having to reinterpret your own experience. This can be scary. A 'defensive' person cannot afford to expose himself to ideas and views that are different from his own. . . . Kids who have flexible parents respond positively when they see their mothers and fathers willing to change, willing to be human."

The happiness of parent and child hinges on the quality of their communication. And from what we know about the terrible dangers that runaways face in our cities and on our highways, it appears that our children's very *lives* may be riding on the quality of our communication, too.

## PART FOUR

# What to Do
# If Something Happens

# 15

# *What to Do if Your Child Disappears*

Slow down. Consciously replace the incipient panic you feel with an absolute conviction that you *will* find this child.

If the child has disappeared from home, thoroughly search the house and surrounding property. That includes basement nooks and favorite hideouts.

If you have no luck, immediately contact the police. Request that a city, state, and county alarm be sent out and that the missing child's statistics (including fingerprints) be entered into the FBI's National Crime Information Center (NCIC) computer in Washington. Have ready all information to give the police: an up-to-date photograph (and videotape if possible), recent dental charts, fingerprint card, notations of birthmarks and other features, and so on.

If the local police refuse to enter the information in the NCIC, or if they say they have a waiting period before starting an investigation (often it's twenty-four hours), go directly to your local FBI office. Inform them that you've seen the local police and that they've failed to take the report. The FBI is required by law to make the entry at the request of the parent.

When you sit down with investigators try to think what probably happened. Could it have been a noncustodial parental abduction? Do you think your child ran away? If neither of these is likely, could he simply be lost? Sometimes a parent will *say* his child has been kidnapped, even if he thinks his child really ran away. To have run away seems an indictment of the parents. Child-search expert Sergeant Joseph St. John of the Indianapolis Police is so good at what he does that he can pretty much tell, just from interviewing the parents, whether it's an abduction case or a runaway. "Last summer," he says, "I had four separate cases of young girls, eight or nine years old, who stayed out all night. . . . Girls that age don't stay out all night. It was clear right there that something was wrong. In two cases it was sexual abuse at home [that led to this temporary running away]; in two other cases it was physical abuse."

It can sometimes retard an investigation not to level with the police about the circumstances of your child's disappearance. Another child-search specialist, Patrick Mulligan, has found that "the profile of a child who may have run away [is different from that of] the child who may have been stolen"; and there may be different techniques for finding them.

Tell the investigators everything you know about your child. Don't hold back anything that may be pertinent. If, for instance, your youngster happens to be gay, this is the wrong time to try to suppress that information. In such a case, says Patrick Mulligan, you must proceed cautiously. To plaster a gay district of town with posters and the mention of a big reward could, he says, "drive the child away from those people who may be supporting him in the street. . . . He will then leave what tenuous relationships he has and go even further underground. A runaway doesn't want a *reward* to be what precipitates his returning home. There's a betrayal issue here." Also, of course, if investigators never learn that the youngster is gay, they may not look in the gay district to begin with.

Stay organized. As hours turn into days, continue holding it all together. Write down everything that you have already done—names of people you have contacted, places you have searched. Try to learn of other places your child has frequented.

Contact friends and neighbors. Tell them what has happened and enlist their help. When Dr. Rattray's four-year-old boy David was abducted, the strong support of the neighbors helped get everyone through the ordeal.

Try to find out if anyone else in the area is missing. Possibly they are together.

Check area hospitals, medical examiners, bus stations, airports, etc.

Inspect your phone bills for the past several months. Unusual calls may be a tip-off of a runaway plan or may have other useful implications.

If you have a strong feeling that your child's been abducted, immediately get an extra phone line installed in the house. Don't let the phone company tell you they'll do it in two weeks. Right away. In the meantime, try to keep the phone lines open as much as possible. When using the phone, wait approximately five minutes between calls, in case someone is trying to contact you.

Ask the police to check the Department of Motor Vehicles and other agencies that might have information about your youngster's activities.

If any calls come in demanding a ransom, notify the police immediately so that they can bring in the FBI. Even without a ransom demand, the FBI can be on the case quickly. After twenty-four hours, the crossing of state lines (one FBI criterion for entering a case) can be presumed.

Contact nonprofit organizations in your area that will help you. Groups such as Child Find are all around the nation and many offer their services without charge. The Adam Walsh Child Resource Center in Fort Lauderdale, Florida, and the National Center for Missing and Exploited Children in Washington, D.C., are mines of immediately useful information.

If the case is not solved within a day, it would be a good

idea to make up posters with your child's photograph on it and the telephone number of the police and/or FBI. Some people advise parents not to put their own home phone number on the poster because there are often crank calls. Consult with the police as to whether you want to put your child's last name on the poster. There's a difference of opinion on the advisability of this.

Enlist neighbors and townspeople to help put up posters, conduct search parties, etc. The object is to get the word out about your child, so don't hesitate to contact the local TV and radio stations as well as area newspapers. Sergeant Joseph St. John has often benefited from his good relationship with the media. He tries to pick his shots carefully. For instance, Indianapolis has a large black population, and if the missing child is black, he may enlist the help of the big soul station in town. If it's a white kid he may contact the country music station. If it's an ongoing investigation, he may resort to the newspapers. Not long ago a one-month-old premature baby was abducted. "We knew who had it, but we just couldn't find him. . . . It happened just before the ten o'clock news time, so I had the perfect opportunity to get it on fresh." As it happened the infant was recovered through other means, but he feels that the TV report was a terrific backup, in case other methods hadn't worked.

Watch out for psychics. Some distraught parents bring them in as a last resort. Sometimes these people just volunteer. At one point, recalls John Walsh bitterly, as many as sixty psychics were working on his son Adam's case. "Every one but one said Adam was alive. That's their batting average. Revé worked with them. She had to do something to keep herself busy, and they were giving her hope. Ghoulish."

Likewise, be careful about private detectives. For the most part they have no better access to information than the police have. In fact, they usually *go* to the police to find out what's happening. "I know cases where they took families for about $30,000," says Richard Ruffino. In one case, he says, "a nonprofit group located the kid. And the detective called up that group and said, 'What right did you have to interfere with my case?' . . . Now why would a guy make a phone call like that? Because his source of income was cut off!"

Ruffino has seen detectives charging $350 a day plus expenses, and in one case $550 a day. This last one, he says, "calls himself a 'forensic investigator,' which is a very fancy title. What he does is track down dead people and match them up with those who are missing." But the guy couldn't even read dental charts, scoffs Ruffino. "Rip-off! Bloodsucker!"

Nevertheless, he says, there are some good private investigators, and with police reluctance to go after runaways or parentally abducted kids, it may become necessary to hire this sort of assistance. In many cases, "If you want an answer, you've got to buy one."

But first, advises Ruffino, give the police a chance to do their job. "It's an awesome responsibility to locate someone who's missing, and the answers don't come as fast as you would want them. Be patient."

Not passively patient, of course. Keep in touch with the investigation, and without getting in their hair or in their way, make the police keep you informed of developments.

If you think the investigation isn't being handled properly, ask to see the chief law-enforcement officer (usually the police chief) and discuss the matter with him. Meanwhile, continue all your other efforts. Searching for a lost child is like launching a small industry: you may feel like you're juggling twenty balls at once. Then suddenly there may seem nothing to do at all but wait.

During the frenetic as well as the down times, it is especially important to support one another in the family. Try not to fly off the handle with one another, despite the pressure. You need family support now more than ever.

# 16

# *What to Do if Your Child Is Molested*

Molestation can mean so many things, from a furtive feel and a lewd remark to a brutal rape, that one has to be careful about generalizing. It's also presumptuous to advise anyone about how to react. You will feel what you feel and do what you have to do. Outrage and disbelief are two common first reactions, and they're entirely understandable.

But perhaps just this much advice would be useful, for your child's sake: feel the outrage, but don't disbelieve. Many children are *retraumatized* by their parents' reactions. It's not easy, after all, for a child to tell his parents what has happened. Then to be called a liar is to be brutalized yet again.

Children seldom lie about these things. One police department in Michigan gave lie-detector tests a few years ago to children who claimed to have been molested because the men accused in those cases claimed vehemently that the kids were lying. Of the 148 children tested, 147 passed the polygraph test with no difficulty. In the 148th case the results were ambiguous.

If the children are very young, how could they lie? They haven't the vocabulary or the concepts with which to construct such a fabrication. And why would they want to lie when they know it will only get them into trouble? Those few cases in which a child does lie—keeps changing his story, for instance—are so remarkable as to raise warning flags that something else is amiss. A little girl, though traumatized by her experience, may want to protect the molester, especially if he happens to be someone she loves, like her father. Or she may lie because her molester has threatened to kill her parents and burn down the house if she tells. Pedophiles will do what they can to procure a child's silence, and terrorizing the child is as effective a means as any.

So whatever your child says, *receive* it. Listen openly and actively. Now is the moment to hold back the rage and hysteria and to be as accepting as you can of what your child is saying. After all, she or he is the victim, not you. Try to be sure you understand exactly what your child is saying. In this respect Dr. Thomas Gordon's ideas on parental effectiveness training can be very helpful. Decoding a child's message may not be easy at first because he's likely to speak elliptically about the experience he's just been through. Feed back to the child what he's saying to check if you've gotten it right. Communicate acceptance, both of him and of his efforts to tell you what's on his mind; and keep the door open so that he'll feel encouraged to go on and tell you more.

Recent crime segments on WNEW-TV's "10 O'Clock News" on Channel 5 in New York gave helpful suggestions on how to do this. Dr. Georgette Bennett arranged a role-playing exchange between a six-year-old boy and author Dr. Carol Flax. David, the little boy, began first:

DAVID: My uncle's annoying me.
FLAX: You know how your uncle is. He's just playful.
DAVID: It's very annoying.
FLAX: That's the way he is. You can accept him the way he is. Go out and play with your friends.
DAVID: Fine.

"A perfect example," comments Dr. Bennett, "of how *not* to listen. David's signal, his cry for help, was ignored." They tried it again:

> DAVID: My uncle's annoying me.
> FLAX: Your uncle's annoying you. Tell me what seems to be bothering you.
> DAVID: He keeps touching me.
> FLAX: He keeps touching you and this is bothering you. Have you spoken to Uncle about this?
> DAVID: Yes.
> FLAX: You *have* spoken to Uncle about this? And Uncle's reaction was . . . ?
> DAVID: He won't stop.
> FLAX: He won't stop.
> DAVID: And he's touching me all over. He's touching and he's not stopping.
> FLAX: He's touching in places that make you feel uncomfortable. Okay. We'll have to talk to Uncle about this.

Well, it's not Harold Pinter, but this scrap of dialogue can teach us something about listening. First, it's important to catch the *opening signal,* in this case David's coded statement: "My uncle's annoying me."

That could mean anything at all. You want to *check the listening* and keep the door open. Use the same words as the child to make sure you understand: "Your uncle's annoying you."

Then explore that signal to *find out the feelings* behind it: "Tell me what seems to be bothering you."

That allows the *hidden information* to come out: "He's touching and he's not stopping."

Now the parent is in a position to *do* something to help: "We'll have to talk to Uncle about this."

Verbal signals are not the only indicators for parents to pay attention to. Sexually abused kids of any age group may complain of pain in the genitals. For preschoolers parents should be alert to signs of redness about the genitals or infections that might be caused by venereal disease. They should be concerned about *preschoolers* who suddenly have sleeping problems; a change in eating habits; uncharacteristic bed-wetting; fearfulness of strangers, especially men, when there'd been no such fear before; or any overtly sexual behavior, such as little girls masturbating frequently.

With *school-age* but still prepubescent children, symptoms may include a drop in school performance; marked changes in social behavior, such as withdrawing from other kids, or, on the other hand, an uncharacteristic aggressiveness toward them; or a sudden shyness with strangers, especially men.

With *adolescents*, sexual abuse could trigger a precipitous drop in academic performance; a withdrawal from peers; signs of venereal disease or pregnancy. One study found evidence of severe depression and drug and/or alcohol abuse in 75 percent to 90 percent of adolescent incest victims.

MEDICAL EXAMINATION

In most cases, if you've determined that your child has been sexually abused, it's important to bring him or her in for a thorough medical examination. Bruises or cuts should be treated and evaluated and all bodily orifices examined for injuries and/or for the presence of semen. If appropriate, it's a good idea to test for venereal disease.

Most physicians are required to report sexual assaults on children to the police, regardless of what the parents do. In the book *Your Children Should Know*, Flora Colao and Tamar Hosansky have a sensitive chapter on this subject. They note that medical procedures tend to be frightening to young children, and especially so if a child has been sexually traumatized. The doctor, they explain, should talk to both parent and child, telling them (in language the child understands) just what's going on. The authors note that pelvic and anal exams are uncomfortable at the best of times and that after a sexual assault they can be unbearably painful.

Children should be allowed to ask whatever questions they want during this whole process and should be warned when something is going to hurt. "It is important to note," say Colao and Hosansky, "that in both types of examinations, the child is often in the same physical position s/he was in when assaulted." In fact, to a nine-year-old (that's the average age for a sexually assaulted child), the exam may be more frightening than the original incident itself. Doctors, nurses, and social workers should be trained to respond to a child's special needs at this time. In many medical facilities the personnel do have some training in child-oriented techniques of examination. At the Sexual Assault Center in Seattle, Washington, doctors sometimes hold the child on their laps rather than examining him or her on the table.

Specialized centers like the one in Seattle or the Child Protection Center—Special Unit in Children's Hospital National Medical Center in Washington, D.C., not only treat the child's physical injuries and test for VD, they also offer counseling for the child and for other members of the family and collect medical evidence in support of investigation and prosecution.

In Seattle the counselors work closely with caseworkers from the state's Children's Protective Services (CPS), which has three main responsibilities: 1) to substantiate reports of child abuse; 2) to develop a plan for dealing with the medical and emotional consequences of the abuse; and 3) to protect the child from further abuse. This might mean (in cases of incest, for instance) petitioning the court for a no-contact order or placing the child outside the home.

The counselors at the Seattle center do not treat offenders, even though they recognize that offenders need help. They feel that to offer such treatment would interfere with their role as advocate for the child. But they do maintain close contact with the offenders' therapists in order to coordinate the family's treatment as a whole and to help with a later reconciliation, if that's what the family wants.

# 17

# How to Deal with the Court System

Most cases of child molestation are never prosecuted, either because the child doesn't tell anyone about it or because the family fears that the judicial process will further traumatize the child. To an extent these fears are justified; after all, even adults can feel shaken up about having to testify in a courtroom. How much worse for a child to face a roomful of strange adults—one of them actually wearing robes!— and to be cross-examined about painfully intimate events that the child may already be feeling ashamed of and guilty about.

Then again, it's important to realize that the molester is counting on just these fears and misgivings on the part of parents. And if he *isn't* taken to court, convicted, and separated from society, he will almost certainly lay hands on other children—probably many other children. Considering the likelihood that some as-yet-unknown proportion of molested children will be so psychologically affected by the experience as to one day become molesters themselves, it is evident how important it is to break the cycle of abuse. That means, on the most basic level, blowing the whistle on these abusers. Stopping them.

Judge Reggie Walton, in Washington, D.C., is well aware

of the difficulties involved in prosecuting these cases. The majority of incidents, he says, go undetected. "If they're detected, you have the difficulty of getting the child to testify. If you get the child to testify, you have the problem of convincing a jury." Most adults, he says, don't want to believe what the child is saying.

He remembers the case of a three-year-old girl that came to his attention about six years ago. She was the youngest of three sisters. The oldest, then twenty-two, had been molested most of her life. The middle child, age fourteen, seemed also to have been molested, though she wouldn't talk about it. And now the three-year-old. "So it was like seventeen years of molesting by the father before it was ever brought to anyone's attention," says Judge Walton.

Would a jury believe a three-year-old? "Well, I don't know. *I* believed her; and had she been able to open up, others would have believed her. . . . I don't believe a girl that age would have been astute enough to make up that story. She finally told me about it, just her and I in my office talking. About her father taking out what she called his 'ding-a-ling' and telling her it was her bottle. And he'd have her commit oral sex."

But though the girl was able to tell Judge Walton about it in private, she was too afraid to tell her story in court. So the man was acquitted. His wife took him back, even though she knew what he was doing to the children. He was a good provider, she told the judge, and if she left him she'd end up on welfare.

There were three problems, then, affecting this case. The three-year-old (understandably) was terrified of having to tell her story over and over again to frightening grown-ups; the oldest sister, then twenty-two, could not testify because too much time had elapsed under the statute of limitations; and the mother chose moral blinders and economic expediency over the psychological welfare of her own children.

Public understanding of child abuse is growing and public outrage mounting, and there may soon be laws in Washington, D.C., and elsewhere *extending* the statute of limitations in child-abuse cases; permitting *videotaping* of a child's testimony so that he or she doesn't have to appear in court; mandating *vertical prosecution* so that one cast of characters rather than several is involved, thus sparing a child many painful retellings of the story; and disseminating *public information* about the possible long-term consequences of child sexual abuse. Perhaps the mother would have thought twice about bringing the abuser back home if she'd known what that might do to her daughters. In any case none of these measures was in place, and the three-year-old must be nine or ten now. "I would suspect she might have been molested this entire time," says Judge Walton.

If a child is willing and able to testify it is essential that nothing be held back. Another case to come before Judge Walton involved an eight-year-old girl, and this time the case was lost because the mother withheld evidence. What appears to have happened is that the mother's boyfriend approached the little girl as she was getting ready to go off to school. While she was still in her nightclothes he fondled her, got on top of her, and ejaculated over her underwear and nightgown. The girl told her mother the next day and turned over the semen-stained clothes. But in an apparent panic of willful disbelief the woman hid the evidence for eight months. By the time the clothes were turned over to the FBI for analysis, the spermatozoa had broken down to such an extent that the lab technicians could not say definitively that it was human semen. The defense attorney argued vigorously that since there was a male cat in the house, it could have been the cat that had caused the semen stains. The contention seems farfetched, but it created a "reasonable doubt" in the minds of the jury, and the man was acquitted.

Officer Dennis Cullen of the Philadelphia Police Department's Sex Crimes Unit agrees that total honesty—by child and parent—is essential if a prosecution is to be successful. This is not easy, which is why Judge Walton stresses the importance of having prosecutors and police officers who are accustomed to working with children. "If the child feels comfortable with the prosecutor who's presenting the case," he says, "and with the officer who's investigating the case, it's going to make for a better presentation when the case comes to trial."

In cases of sexual abuse the child is usually the only witness to the crime, and it's therefore essential that he or she be an effective witness. Criminologist Dr. Georgette Bennett sometimes finds herself asked to testify in trials and she suggests the following:

1. Listen closely to what is being asked.
2. Answer only the question that is being asked.
3. Try to answer simply. Sometimes a plain "Yes" or "No" will do. Volunteer nothing or you may be defeating the examining lawyer's efforts to make a crucial point.
4. Tell the truth. It's a crime not to. But, says Dr. Bennett, "telling the truth is more than just speaking words. The judge and jury will be watching your body language to see if it belongs to your words. So I always make sure I sit relaxed. And I make eye contact with the jury, the lawyer, and the judge."

For a little child it's sometimes permitted to have a grown-up friend in court, someone he or she can relate the story to if it's too scary to look around at the judge and jury. That way the testimony can seem more like a personal, one-to-one conversation. It can help the child relax; and that, of course, makes the child's testimony all the more convincing.

One day perhaps all law-enforcement organizations will have specially trained units who know how to deal sensitively with child witnesses, before, during, and after the trial itself. But this costs money and (an even scarcer commodity) it takes imagination. Philadelphia is one city that

has a special unit. Officer Dennis Cullen, for instance, has
had special sensitivity training for working with kids. And
he takes his time with them. "I talk with the kid about
innocuous things at first, just to get them to realize that
we're human. A lot of parents routinely scare their children
by telling them, 'If you're bad, I'll call the cops and have
you arrested.' So kids may be afraid of us. I show them
pictures of my own kids, so they know that I'm a father."

With very small children the police sometimes use anatomically correct dolls, getting the kids, during play sessions, to *show* what happened to them. Older children, of
course, must be more verbal, but they can use whatever
words they would normally. "They don't have to impress us
with their knowledge of biology," says Cullen. "If they call
it a 'tinkler,' it's a tinkler, and I don't correct them. If a girl
says, 'He touched my tinkler,' I may say, 'Well, where is
your tinkler?' And she will indicate it's between her legs."

In Philadelphia the grand jury is not invoked, but the
child has to tell the story several times, first to the investigating officer, then to the district attorney's child-abuse
unit, then to a judge at the preliminary hearing. If the case
goes to trial the child may have to tell it again to another
judge. The Pennsylvania legislature is currently mulling
over a bill to allow videotaping of a child's statement so that
he or she can be spared a courtroom confrontation with the
alleged molester. There are constitutional difficulties to be
ironed out here, but Cullen thinks it would make prosecution of these cases a lot less traumatic for the child—and it
would get a permanent early record of the child's description of what happened. This is important since it can sometimes be a year or more between the start of a case and its
being brought to trial.

Until such reforms are instituted the police will have to
depend on the bravery of small children. They often have
additional help, oddly enough, from the molesters themselves. A lot of these characters photograph the children

and keep detailed records and diaries of their sexual acts. "I'm not talking about photos of kids playing in the school yard," says Officer Cullen. "These are sexually explicit photographs." Quite often there are a number of children shown in such pictures. The police immediately get a warrant, seize all the documentary material they can, try to identify and contact other children in the pictures, and if possible get complaints by these others as well. All this makes the case a lot stronger than it would otherwise be.

Even so, the pedophile, out on bail, will do whatever he can to keep the case from coming to trial. Sometimes he'll approach the child's parents and offer them money not to prosecute. "A lot of these parents are from lower economic backgrounds to begin with," says Officer Cullen, "so money can be a strong inducement." Sometimes, he says, it was money that got the kids to go along with the molester in the first place.

If that doesn't work the pedophile may try other tactics, including getting some other kids to threaten the testifying child. He may have them go up to the kid and say, "Don't testify or we're going to beat you up." By doing this through other kids the pedophile can often avoid being accused of trying to intimidate the witness.

So, yes, it does take a lot of courage to bring charges against a pedophile. But children are often remarkably brave. Officer Cullen has recently been working with an eight-year-old girl who was snatched and raped by a burly six-foot-four man from Cherry Hill, New Jersey. She was very withdrawn afterward, recalls Cullen, and for two weeks wouldn't tell what had happened. Finally he was able to draw the story from her. Immediately he realized that she was feeling guilty and ashamed and so he "took that guilt off of her," explaining that it was not in any way her fault, any more than it would be if the man had stolen her money. Once she told him the story she felt relieved and agreed to go ahead and testify. When the preliminary hearing came up, there she was, a tiny girl on the witness stand, and sitting seven or eight feet away from her, the huge frightening man who had hurt her. The contrast, says Cullen, "helped the prosecution, but it terrified her." Nevertheless, the little girl persevered and told the story straight out. "She did a great job," beams Cullen. "She was a real trooper."

It's important for parents to recognize that as vulnerable as young children are and as traumatized as they can sometimes be by the actions of pedophiles, they also have a highly developed sense of justice. They want the bad man punished, just as they are punished when *they* do something bad. And they particularly don't want this man going out and doing to other kids what he did to them. Parents, in their natural urge to protect children from possible further traumatization, should take account of this strong need on the part of many children to see justice done. And they should also realize that—thank God—children are often a great deal braver and more resilient than we give them credit for being.

# 18

# *How to Help Your Child Afterward*

Late afternoon on the boardwalk. We're watching the high-tide ocean scrambling over the weedy shore. Snatches of rain in the wind. Pam Rattray talks about the aftermath of her son David's kidnapping. The first day after he was rescued he was jumping and tumbling about the house for joy, she says. The second day he veered over into hysterics—totally uncontrollable. Chuck Rattray just picked his son up and plunked him into a tub of hot water and got in with him and held him. The two of them stayed there a long time, talking and crying it out together.

"David was a lot better after that," says Pam. He's become more aggressive, though, than he was before the kidnapping. He used to be quite shy; now he'll make more insistent demands. He clings more than he used to. And, not surprisingly, he's afraid of the dark. Three days bound and gagged in a car trunk would make anyone terrified of the dark.

"He's reluctant to go upstairs by himself if it's dark," says Dr. Rattray. Often he sleeps downstairs in his parents' bedroom.

Yes, one can understand David's fear of spending the night in his big beautiful upstairs room. At night a lazy ceiling fan scratches around and around, slicing shadows; and outside the white wooden shutters, the shadows of leaves move continually about. There's much that is reassuring about David's room: the stuffed animals (a Garfield hand puppet perched on the bedpost); inscribed pictures of heroes like Fernando Valenzuela and Manny Mota of the L.A. Dodgers; the bathroom wallpaper covered with pictures of football helmets; a blue plastic Cookie Monster chair and a yellow plastic Big Bird chair . . . all the magical paraphernalia of childhood. But still, the darkness. Even with the light on in the hall, night insinuates itself into every corner. And, like the other members of the family, David still has occasional nightmares about the abduction.

The Rattrays have dealt with David's fears and increased aggressiveness without resorting to psychiatrists or counselors. They'll sit down and talk with him about the incident, but only if he signals in some way that he wants to. "We want to do what he wants to do," says Dr. Rattray. "We don't want to make a special issue of it."

Many families don't want to talk about their children's abduction—they want to forget that it happened—and so the kids don't get a chance to work out the complex feelings they may still be in the grip of. Talking is important because often a child doesn't realize how much rage he really has in him until he starts talking about it.

David's mother, Pamela, is not sorry to see him expressing more anger nowadays than in the past. "I'm glad to see it coming out now instead of when he's twenty-five. Then he might not know why."

So David decides when to talk about the ordeal and when not to. Sometimes he'll ask about the man who took him. He's not happy to be told that the man's still alive. He'd prefer him dead. David's afraid he might come back and steal him again. Chuck and Pamela Rattray explain to him that the man shot himself accidentally in the head and is not likely to go anywhere ever again. He can apparently perform certain simple functions, like raising a spoon to his lips, but he may never be competent to stand trial.

What the Rattrays did when their son returned home from his ordeal was surround him with love and keep open all lines of communication with him so that he knew he could talk about the incident whenever he chose to. Also, the whole family enrolled in a beginner's karate class. It was held on an inconvenient night for the doctor, and after a while the family stopped going; but David loved it and regained much of the self-esteem that had been stripped from him. After all, he had not only been terrorized, he had been humiliated. There were no trips to a bathroom, no warm showers. Tied up in the trunk, he had been forced to foul his own clothes. Now he could punch and kick and leap about on the mats getting out his anger.

The family loves their little Chihuahua named Buford and their tiny Boston terrier named Baby, but after David's ordeal, some more imposing canine seemed in order. Hence, Bark Vader, an enormous, frightening black German shepherd who can scare the pants off (or *tear* the pants off) anyone who comes into the house. Still, he's loving and patient with David and his nine-year-old sister Laurie Ann.

"We don't beat Vader if he snaps at somebody," says Dr. Rattray. "Vader's here for protection." David feels a lot safer knowing that.

After being reduced to total helplessness it's important that the returning child-victim be "reempowered" in as many ways as possible. David was helped by learning some strategies for avoiding kidnapping in the future.

Walking along the Vero Beach boardwalk, with a slap of wet warm wind in our faces, Pamela Rattray explains that some months after David's kidnapping a sixteen-year-old Vero Beach girl was abducted, raped, and murdered. After that, she says, the schools instituted safety programs and advised children how to protect themselves. In David's pre-kindergarten class the teacher was talking about not ever getting in a car with a stranger. "And she said—I don't think she realized what she was saying—'Don't ever come if a stranger calls to you.' Well, David's head just dropped."

He was feeling ashamed, Pam thinks, because he *did* come when the man called to him to come inside the house. The four-year-old David was then tied and gagged and kidnapped. "He feels if only he'd run straight over to the neighbors' house, all that wouldn't have happened."

It's common for children to blame themselves for their own victimization, even if there was little they could have done to prevent it. David is lucky. Not only does he have a warm and supportive family around him; he also escaped wounding, mayhem, and the horrors of sexual assault. There, too, the victim-survivor often blames himself. The rest of the family blame themselves as well. It's a feeling that's hard to get over.

Back in February 1982 in Concord, California, three-year-old Tara Burke was ripped from the arms of her nine-year-old brother, Jeremy, as they sat in the car waiting for their parents to come out of a store. Jeremy fought fiercely to protect his sister and when that didn't work he ran into the store and got his mother. Too late. Months passed with no clue to Tara's whereabouts. Tara's father, Steven Burke, a blind piano tuner, and his wife, Liz, lived during that time in what must have seemed a different element than mere air; it was the rarefied ozone of terror. At last, after ten unlivable months, they heard great news, terrible news: Tara was found alive in the back of a van, where she'd been held captive and had been sexually abused with great regularity. An eleven-year-old Vietnamese boy who'd been held captive with her escaped through a vent in the van's roof and ran for help.

Coming home was not easy. Even two years later Tara seems confused about why the kidnappers are in jail and she isn't. She has developed a fear of strangers that may never completely leave her. At first it is said she wanted to have nothing to do with her brother, Jeremy, who hadn't been able to prevent her kidnapping. That reaction, of course, threw poor Jeremy into a tailspin, since he'd already been feeling terribly guilty. His behavior apparently became obstreperous in school and he was sent to see a counselor.

Counseling is essential in cases like this. And of course Tara herself received therapy. Her therapist used dolls to help her express some of the things her abductors had done to her. Tara had changed a lot during her ordeal, and on her return she'd scream and carry on if she didn't get her way.

Her mother, at first, did not encourage Tara to talk about her experience, but the counselor said that, no, it was important for the child to express all those things and work through them. It was tough to listen to it, though. What mother wants to hear about the physical and sexual abuse of her little girl?

And so, gradually, through continuing couseling, the Burke family is putting itself back together again. Tara is getting to be almost her old self once more, although she's warier now. When she reaches puberty—a time of confusion for any youngster—she may need more therapy. That's true of many kids who've been roughly initiated into sex many years before they're physically or psychologically ready for it. Even further therapy may be needed when the child is perhaps eighteen or nineteen and has entered into a voluntary sexual relationship. Often people who've been molested as children have trouble handling sexual intimacy later. Sometimes they have flashbacks that poison present pleasures and threaten future happiness.

According to Dr. Sandra Kaplan, chief of child and adolescent psychiatry at North Shore Hospital in Manhasset, New York, the rate of "success" in therapy is much greater in cases of physical abuse than with sexual abuse. Dr. Kaplan is speaking now of abuse within the home, not of abductions. If the family can be brought into therapy, she says, the physical mistreatment of the child can usually be halted. Both child and parents can be made to understand why the beatings or the neglect took place, and a new start can be made.

With sexual abuse in the home, though, it's a lot more difficult. Fathers or stepfathers who have been molesting their daughters are "initially very resistant to treatment," says Dr. Kaplan; "and they're also resistant to accepting responsibility and acknowledging the sexual behaviors that they had with their daughter. It seems to me that until they do that, there's no way the child will ever be able to trust him again."

In most father-daughter incest cases, says Dr. Kaplan, the mother knew what was going on—or at least had an inkling. So there is usually a betrayal issue here with the daughter that has to be worked out before the family can function again. The problem is compounded by the fact that when the mother finds out "it's almost universal that she blames the daughter [for the incest] rather than the husband."

And if this doesn't make it hard enough on the girl, her brothers and sisters usually blame her too. It's her fault that the father has had to leave the house. "They miss the father, and also there are great financial hardships when the father leaves home," says Dr. Kaplan. "Especially if the father is incarcerated."

Family therapy at North Shore for incest cases often takes a good two years. The girl is counseled individually at first, and is treated very supportively. After all, it's hard to imagine a person in a more difficult psychological position: a victim who is blamed by everyone around her and by herself as well. The mother is also treated separately in the beginning, to make her understand the guilt trip she is making her daughter bear. "We work very hard to get the mother to accept the fact that the responsibility [for what happened] lies with the adults."

Individual therapy is also arranged for the father, whether he's in prison or simply living away from the home.

When a certain amount of progress has been made, the therapists work with the mother and father together in an effort to get them to accept their parental responsibility and understand the family dynamics that led to the incest. Then the mother and daughter meet together to attempt to re-establish the daughter's shattered trust in the mother. "And then the last thing we do, if the father has acknowledged his responsibility, is introduce the father into the family therapy sessions."

A key element here is that the father must apologize to the daughter. It is a key that incestuous fathers cannot often bring themselves to turn, which is why many fathers never are reintegrated into the home. If the father is genuinely sorry and vows never to let it happen again, is he "cured"? Dr. Kaplan does not use that term. "The perversion may persist," she says, "but the father has to develop control over it."

Whether the sexual abuse is in the nuclear family, the extended family, or the neighborhood, the offender is almost always someone who has been in a position of trust with regard to the child. Therefore perhaps the main long-term effect of sexual abuse is to make it very difficult for the child to trust anyone completely ever again. Without immediate and intensive therapy the child may never regain that ability to trust, and so may later enter into mistrustful, unhealthy, abusive adult relationships.

There is also the danger, as we've mentioned before, that as the child grows to adulthood he may try to gain control over what happened to him by acting it out with younger, smaller, more vulnerable people than himself. The child may, in other words, become a child molester himself.

Irving Prager, an attorney and children's rights activist, is convinced that there is no known cure for the adult pedophile, but he strongly advocates immediate therapy for the child victim before his victimization becomes "set" into an orientation. In fact, he says, "the mental health profession should strongly support and implement the reallocation of resources previously directed at ineffective experimental treatment for molesters to programs devoted to effective treatment of victims" (*Journal of Juvenile Law*, Vol. 6, 1982, p. 78).

One may dispute his conclusions about molesters and strongly agree with him about the treatment of child victims. In fact, abused children have often lost more than one easily realizes. Not only have they been deprived of their sexual innocence, they have, in a real sense, been deprived of that magical and highly perishable commodity known as childhood.

"They're going to be missing completely certain important [developmental steps]," says Kathleen Kennelly, Community Education Coordinator at the Sexual Assault Center, located in the Harborview Medical Center in Seattle, Washington. "So even when the abuse ends, these kids find that they don't have any friends, and they don't feel like other kids, and they don't know how to [feel close to people]. It's typical for a child who's been molested to become emotionally retarded at the age when the molesting started. If it started when he was six and was discovered when he was ten, we may find out that . . . emotionally he's still back at six."

Another dangerous aftereffect has to do with the premature sexualization of the child. Many victimized kids may start acting out seductive or sexualized forms of behavior. When you start doing this in the school yard or when the family gathers at Thanksgiving, it's going to cause a lot of confusion, embarrassment, and even social ostracism. "A young girl may come up to an adult male," says Ms. Kennelly, "and touch his genital area or make some other kind of sexual gesture. Clearly, it's important for that adult male to let her know not to do that—'I'd like to give you a hug and put my arm around you, but we don't touch in *that* way.' "

This is, of course, putting all adult males on the honor system not to take advantage of this victim who seems to be begging to be further victimized. Such a girl needs immediate therapy, and her parents need guidance as well, so that they know what to watch for. "If they see their child at thirteen starting to behave destructively or to exhibit a real negative self-image, they should know that that is probably related to the sexual abuse"—even if the abuse took place years earlier. Parents need help, at such times, sorting out what are normal things for a teenager to do and what are not normal actions, perhaps sparked by the molestation.

We wince when we see woodland brutally cleared for some crass new development. How much more brutal it must be when the delicate ecology of childhood is overturned by an intrusive and premature sexuality. After such bulldozing all sorts of strange and uncataloged plant forms are likely to spring up. And even if the molestation ceases, how long it is before the land is reclaimed by trees and flowers, and how long before childhood can be felt again in a child's heart.

Kathleen Kennelly, at Seattle's Sexual Assault Center, sees a very hopeful sign: "We see younger and younger children who are molested for shorter and shorter periods of time," she says, "because there's a much greater awareness about sexual abuse and children are being taught now to tell about it. That's very positive."

It used to be years, even decades, before children dared tell about sexual abuse. Now it may be days or weeks. That is a great bit of news, because the shorter the duration of the abuse, the greater the likelihood that the child will recover from it completely and still have some portion of his childhood that will actually feel like childhood.

That is why it is so essential to push on with public information about these issues. An informed and aroused citizenry will be able to recognize the signs of abuse quickly, move to separate the molester from society decisively, and start the victim's recovery process immediately. This is the only way the multigenerational cycle of psychic destruction and despair can be broken and our children healed.

## PART FIVE

# The Broader Issues

# 19

# The Controversy: Punishment vs. Rehabilitation

"The hell with psychiatric care! Just shove that turkey somewhere and let the guys in the prison play with him for a while!" That's the reaction of one father after learning that his little daughter had been photographed in pornographic poses and molested by the administrator of the day-care center she attended.

Patti Linebaugh, founder of a national organization called SLAM (Society's League Against Molesters), might not put it quite that way, but she'd sympathize with the sentiment. She's extremely impatient with the idea that pedophiles can be rehabilitated through psychiatric treatment. A number of prisons have voluntary sex-offender therapy programs. The State Correctional Institution in Somers, Connecticut, for instance, has about 150 men participating in such a program, and Dr. William Hobson (one of the doctors who runs it) feels it has helped cut down the recidivism rate. In other words, of prisoners eventually released from Somers, those molesters who participated in the treatment program were less likely to commit similar crimes again than those who did not take part in the program.

For Patti Linebaugh "less likely" is not enough. Not that she believes released molesters are *any* less likely to repeat their offenses. As for Dr. Hobson's claims, she says, "Of course that's his profession and his job."

Molesters, while in prison, may *seem* to respond to therapy, but she thinks they don't molest kids there only because there are no kids around. "Unless they're outpatients," she says. "Theodore Frank was an outpatient who'd been in and out of treatment programs for years. Six weeks after he was released as a model patient, totally rehabilitated, he killed my granddaughter. Two and a half years old. Amy Sue was sadistically raped and sodomized. Her breasts were torn off with vise grips, and she had lateral lacerations on her body. *This* was the result of a treatment program."

A worse horror story is impossible to imagine. But what do you do with convicted pedophiles?

"I feel you should lock them away forever. . . . I feel very strongly that at this time there is not anything available that prevents child molestation. You can put it in the same category as homosexuality. Or you can put it in the category of heterosexuality. You take a heterosexual and tell him, 'Okay, you're going to change your sexual desires. Instead of loving your wife, you're going to love someone of your same sex.' Do you think that would work? It is *not* a sickness. It is a sexual desire."

Irving Prager agrees. A West Coast attorney and legislative activist, he successfully prosecuted Theodore Frank and helped set up SLAM (originally called Concerned Citizens for Stronger Legislation Against Child Molesters). Prager doesn't think therapy helps molesters. He doesn't think anybody has yet discovered a way to change their behavior, and he can be sarcastic about those who claim they have.

"If you ask, 'What can you cure better, child molestation or robbery?' the answer is robbery. I think they should redirect their efforts. They should have robbery-treatment centers, burglary-treatment centers, forgery-treatment centers. But *never* something so difficult to change as sexual orientation."

Sometimes psychiatrists try "aversion therapy" (e.g., administering electric shocks or noxious odors to molesters while they're being shown child pornography). Ineffective, he says. And in the few places where it's been tried in its extreme forms the courts have stopped it as cruel and unusual punishment. If it did work, says Prager, it should really be applied to all sorts of criminals. "If you were a forger, we'd take you into a room and show you a check, and every time you saw the check we'd hit you over the head with a two-by-four. After doing this for about a week you'd stop forging. Every time you saw a checkbook you'd get sick."

Prager's derisive description makes the notion sound comical. In fact, psychiatrists now generally agree that aversion therapy, at least by itself, is ineffective—"unless it was taken to such a Pavlovian extent that you became deranged." But the American justice system, rightly, is reluctant to get into the business of brainwashing.

What about Depo-Provera or other new drugs that take away the sex drive? Not long ago Roger A. Gauntlett, an heir to the huge Upjohn chemical company, was convicted in Kalamazoo, Michigan, of raping his teenage stepdaughter. He was sentenced to five years probation and what the judge called "chemical castration," which meant he had to take regular doses of Depo-Provera, a drug which, as irony would have it, is produced by Upjohn. There are a couple of problems with that, though. One is that the drug works only as long as you take it; it's not really castration at all. Another problem is that rape and pedophilia are not entirely sexually caused. They have more to do with the issue of power. To reduce the sexual urgency would not be to diminish the hostility. Perhaps the offender won't actually rape his next victim. He might kill her instead.

After public outcry over Gauntlett's light sentence, he was resentenced on September 21, 1984, to five to fifteen years. The public doesn't believe in better living through chemistry.

Okay, but then what about plain old castration?

"Doesn't work," pronounces William Prendergast, director of a treatment program for sex offenders in New Jersey. Pedophilia, he says, "is psychogenic in origin, it's not physical. They can still have the fantasy and the need. The confusion is sex being love, and that sex is the way to please kids." Irving Prager agrees that castration doesn't work, although a few states tried it for a while.

But apart from such narrow areas of agreement, there's a real war between those who, like Prendergast, think pedophiles can be rehabilitated and those who, like Prager, think they can't.

California, until the shock of the Theodore Frank case, was committed to the view that sexual offenders are mentally ill and should be treated as patients, not as criminals. Under the state's Mentally Disordered Sex Offender (MDSO) program, more molesters were hospitalized than were imprisoned. Since 1949 about 1,000 offenders per year were given MDSO treatment, for the most part at Atascadero State Hospital. Theodore Frank was one of the beneficiaries of MDSO. He was thought to have responded so well that after his release he was invited to come back to Atascadero to give a guest lecture. Then his murderous side erupted again and a two-and-a-half-year-old child was tortured to death. In 1981 the California legislature abolished the MDSO program. In its place: mandatory prison sentences.

We may not be able to judge the MDSO program on its real merits because it was never properly staffed or funded. As Prager himself notes in his article, " 'Sexual Psychopathy' and Child Molesters: The Experiment Fails" (*Journal of Juvenile Law*, Vol. 6, 1982, p. 71), "In 1978, only three psychiatrists and two psychologists were on the Atascadero staff to treat 1,000 patients. At Patton State Hospital, 200 MDSOs convicted in California were treated by one psychologist who later observed . . . 'I don't know how you call that treatment.' "

Dr. William Hobson, who works with sex offenders at the maximum-security prison in Somers, Connecticut, provides a glimpse of life on the battlefront: "The best analogy that I make to this place is, it's the mental-health version of 'M*A*S*H.' We're understaffed, we're overworked. It's basically Nick [Dr. A. Nicholas Groth] and myself, both working part-time in the sex-offender program—we have other duties—and so in a sense we have one full-time person. Last semester we had 150 men in our sex-offender program. . . . We do the best we can. We develop certain defense mechanisms . . . we laugh sometimes at things that are not that funny, and we may sometimes sound callous. . . . I'm sure that people might be released before we think they ought to be . . . but we get to the point where we say, 'Hey, we've done all that we can do.' We can't follow people around out there. I can worry, but I would just hope that maybe the court system or the police will be more aware of them, and the court system will deal with them more harshly if it ever occurs again."

Such honesty is not terrifically reassuring to the rest of us. We certainly don't want to *count* on the court system being "more aware" of reoffending child molesters the next time around.

Prager says there shouldn't *be* a next time around. "If you believe that child molesters should continue to be among children, you're the enemy. . . . And anyone in the mental-health field would have to say, 'Hey, the only way we can treat these guys is put them among kids and see if they reoffend.' Well, I'm sorry, that shouldn't be tolerated."

But the alternative, unless we take sex offenders out back and shoot them, is to keep them in prison forever. Problem. We don't have enough prisons, and the public doesn't want to pay the price tag to build a whole bunch more. It costs $21,000 per man to house people in the Avenel, New Jersey, facility. In Somers, Connecticut, it's about $15,000. California's MDSO project was costing $35,000 per person. It's a *lot* of money. We demand that judges throw the book at sex offenders, but we keep voting down bond issues to fund more facilities. Avenel's Adult Diagnostic Center was built for 180 inmates; as of late 1984 it held 297. "Every spare room in this place has become a dormitory," says William Prendergast, "including our basement, which was never made to live in. . . . It's insane. We're warehousing people in a treatment facility."

If society wants to punish these people and put them away for twenty or thirty years, he says, that's okay—but then keep them in a prison, not in a "diagnostic center." As a society we must decide whether we want to treat offenders or just get them out of our hair. One recent New Jersey statute permits a judge to impose a mandatory minimum sentence up to one half of the total (maximum) sentence. If a man is sentenced to forty or fifty years, the judge might give him twenty years mandatory. "The mandatory earns no credits, it's served day for day. So no matter if he stands on his head and transforms into Jesus Christ Superstar, nobody can do anything with him for twenty years! And nobody," says Prendergast, "is in treatment for twenty years. No one *needs* treatment for twenty years. All our programs are aimed at release to the street [and how to cope once one gets out]. What the hell does *he* do for twenty years in group therapy?" Prendergast thinks such people should spend the first seventeen years of the minimum mandatory in a regular prison, and then be brought back to the treatment center for the last three, to be readied psychologically for the real possibility of release.

As it is, only one out of every five sex offenders in New Jersey goes to a treatment facility. Most go to prisons where overcrowding encourages early parole—with no treatment at all.

Avenel's treatment center is unusual in that it's a separate facility—not part of another prison—and treatment is not voluntary. The opposite is true in Somers, where, as Dr.

Hobson reports, "there are a lot of disincentives to participate. . . . To come down here is to risk getting harassment from other inmates."

Avenel's program is also more intensive than an ordinary prison's can be. Each offender is assigned a "primary therapist" who conducts group therapy sessions for one and a half to two hours a week. The "primary" also offers individual therapy, marital therapy, and/or family therapy. There's also "social skills training" (including assertiveness training) and a three-level sex-education course. There's "anger management" for those with problems controlling their rage. There's art therapy, comprising painting, ceramics, even sewing. An education program helps inmates make up for learning deficiencies from grammar-school-level courses through college. And a physical education program works on what Prendergast calls "body-image problems," offering the men weight-lifting and exercise programs as well as intramural sports (which helps them deal with competition and the fear of failure).

This kind of treatment center can be seen as a sort of laboratory where new ideas can be tried out. One fixated pedophile, a difficult case, described to me a special new "masturbatory reconditioning" program he was undergoing in addition to the other therapies. "It's aversion therapy," he says, "and the particular part I'm doing is Satiation. . . . I've done over a hundred hours of it. It isn't permanent, you have to keep after it, but at the moment I can't even get a hard-on to a child." It might be termed masturbating a fantasy to death. "You may go from one fantasy to another till you kill them all," he says.

What this does, says William Prendergast, is "get rid of the deviant fantasy." Permanently? "Oh sure. Of course you're not using it in isolation; you're also doing therapy."

Another type of masturbatory reconditioning, he says, involves "teaching them how to change the fantasy and never again ejaculate to it. So when they reach the point of ejaculatory inevitability they switch over to a positive fantasy. And you teach them how to *make* positive fantasies."

People like Irving Prager out at the La Verne College of Law, or Robert Hect at the Juvenile Justice Center in Washington, D.C., might accuse Prendergast of having "positive fantasies" of his own if he thinks these exercises will actually change habitual sex offenders. "These are the most unrehabilitative criminals there are," says Hect. But at least Prendergast is not one of those who believe that psychotherapy by *itself* can turn molesters into model citizens. Avenel's "whole man approach" combines confrontational therapy sessions (à la Alcoholics Anonymous) with educational and image-improvement activities in an effort to address the complex of psychological factors that led to the aberrant behavior in the first place.

As one inmate, serving a twenty-year sentence for aggravated sexual assault on five boys, told me, "I don't expect to get out of here this year or next year . . . but when the time comes, when the staff does put me up, I feel confident that I have a very very good chance [of not reoffending]. Certainly compared to going to a prison. Because I see already substantial changes in myself."

This sounds pretty good, especially when one hears William Hobson describing the psychic deterioration that can set in after fifteen or twenty years in a regular prison. A child molester by definition has difficulty relating to adults, says Hobson. After fifteen years of being hated and harassed by other inmates, "the guy's going to come out very damaged. And *now* do you think he's going to be able to relate to adults any better?"

Because the truth is, almost all offenders eventually are released. It seems only good sense to release them in the best psychological condition possible.

There is also the fact, as Dr. Fred S. Berlin of the Johns Hopkins Hospital Sexual Disorders Clinic wrote to the Senate Subcommittee on Juvenile Justice in September 1984, that many men who assault children were themselves sexually abused when they were kids. "Thus, in treating a 'victimizer,' one is often in point of fact also treating a former 'victim.' . . . We should not simply write these adults off by relabelling them as victimizers deserving punishment. . . . Data indicates that proper treatment can be effective. Preferably, access to such treatment should be made available early on in life . . . but help needs to be available later on in life as well. Many parents who perhaps understandably are now advocating . . . strong punishment [for molesters] may come to feel quite differently in the future if, God forbid, their own child as a result of premature sexual activities develops a sexual aberration such as pedophilia."

Fair enough. And considering that pedophilia is usually a lifelong inclination, unlike rape and other violent crimes, which tend to taper off when the offender reaches his forties, it's particularly important to find effective treatment for these people.

If there *is* effective treatment. Dr. Berlin says there is. William Prendergast claims that his "whole man" approach is so effective that there's only a 15 percent recidivism rate among Avenel graduates. That figure (at its best) means that fifteen out of every hundred sex offenders released from the facility will later be *convicted* of raping or otherwise damaging other women or children. But very few molesters are convicted, and after one stint in the slammer they may have learned to be more cautious than ever. Prendergast himself talks about one former inmate who was arrested for child molesting nine years after leaving Avenel. That was his first official reoffense; but as the man later admitted, he'd gone back to molesting children just six months after leaving the treatment facility. For the next eight and a half years he was out there hurting kids. "Not only that, but he got a license for a foster home. Don't ask me how, but he did. And those were the kids he was molesting."

William Hobson, at the Somers prison, admits to the un-reliability of statistics. "I've heard statistics that seventy-five percent will eventually reoffend. It's a faulty assumption to think that we know very much with our statistics, because this is the kind of behavior that, let's face it, somebody could do a long time and not get caught."

Some say molesters grab, fondle, or sodomize fifty or sixty children for every conviction. That statistic, like the others, is probably unreliable, but it does put a different complexion on the 15 percent recidivism rate at Avenel. In fact, it could mean that fifteen out of every hundred men released from the facility will eventually molest fifty more kids (or women) each. That's 750 people, or more, traumatized and perhaps permanently harmed for every hundred offenders paroled from a treatment facility. It's as good a statistic as anyone else's.

There is no agreement as to why, if one is sexually abused as a child, one has a tendency in some cases to become an abuser as an adult. Nor is it known what percentage of traumatized children grow up to sexually victimize others. But the fact that there is *some* causal relation between these events is alarming, considering the numbers of children each molester is likely to harm. As Irving Prager writes in the *Journal of Juvenile Law* (Vol. 6, 1982, p. 65), "The release of molesters to again molest *might actually guarantee an incessant increase, of geometric proportion, in the number of child molesters.*" [Emphasis his.]

There may be a useful middle ground to be found between those who argue that child molesters should be put away forever and those who think they can be treated and released, like measles victims, after a brief period of quarantine. William Hobson, a man committed to the mental-health approach, can nevertheless acknowledge that there are some people for whom child abuse is a compulsive chronic behavior; some of these have abused over a thousand kids each. "Those are people who probably need to be locked away and who probably can never change." Others are sadistic, violent people, like Theodore Frank, or the murderer of Adam Walsh. And they, too, should probably never see the outside of a prison wall. What disturbs Hobson is the tendency of the public to "lump together the various categories, putting in the same category child molesters with child rapists with child murderers." Many people convicted of molesting children are capable of being helped, he thinks. The regressed offender, like the father who sexually abuses his teenage daughter at moments of acute stress, may have a good prognosis if given psychological help, perhaps combined with family counseling.

But even in "mild" cases of molestation, legislative activists like Prager feel it's essential to clearly label these offenses *crimes* and to deal with them as such. "The criminal justice system isn't designed to become a therapeutic tool to help troubled individuals." When you attempt to use it that way, he says, "you end up with what we've got today."

What we've got is a crazy quilt of laws in fifty little fiefdoms. In some states molesters tend to be "sentenced" to see a psychiatrist once a week for a certain period of time. But even where there are mandated prison terms the sentence is seldom as long as the mandate decrees. In California, prisoners may serve two thirds of whatever sentence they're given. "If you get six years, you do four," says Prager. In Colorado and other states there's a "good time" provision that takes off one day from your sentence for every day you don't assault a guard or otherwise commit mayhem. Offenders therefore get off after serving as little as half their sentence. But that's not the real problem, says Prager, " 'cause nobody goes to prison in Colorado in the first place."

You can have the toughest laws in the nation, but if judges don't invoke them and prosecutors don't push for the most serious appropriate charge, the laws may as well not be there. Alaska, Arizona, and the state of Washington are said to be in this category. All of them have tough laws—on the books.

Asked to name the ten states with the best (i.e., toughest) laws, Prager responds, "There aren't ten. I wish there were. . . . Utah. California. Colorado. Downhill from there."

Until recently, he says, the worst state was New York, because until mid-1984 New York had a "corroboration requirement." In essence this provision was based on the assumption that women and children usually lie about sexual relations and that therefore the state will not even allow the prosecution of a rapist or molester based solely on a child's or a woman's testimony. There must be independent evidence of the crime. Under the pressure of women's groups, the corroboration rule in New York was abolished as to women, but it was kept for children. Maybe women don't lie so much about sexual relations, but of course children do.

Earlier in this book the case of Hayden Jones was cited as evidence that on occasion a man may be wrongfully convicted of sexual molestation of children. But that is a rare case, and in fact it appears that the children in that case were threatened and beaten—by a police officer, no less—to make them testify against Jones as they did. And they later recanted. What the corroboration rule meant, says Prager, was that in New York (and in Nebraska and Washington, D.C., which also have the rule), "It was open season on kids." After all, since child abuse almost always occurs in secrecy, the child is usually the only witness to the crime. If the child's word is not believed, virtually no cases will be prosecuted. To convict without corroboration, a prosecutor had to show that the offense was forcibly committed—a thing which is hard to prove and which has little bearing on most child-abuse cases, since children often do what they're told without being forced.

"What you need to prosecute a case of this kind with ease are motion pictures of the act, with a clock on the wall, a calendar next to it, and a street sign visible through the window," says Marjory D. Fields, the co-chairman of the governor's commission on domestic violence in New York. According to *The New York Times* (September 22, 1984), 60 percent of child-abuse cases taken to the district attorney in Westchester County, New York, in 1983 could not be prosecuted for lack of corroboration. As to convictions, only two of 145 randomly selected cases brought in New York City from 1975 to 1977 resulted in convictions. This is how we protect our children?

Though the corroboration requirement seems to be on the way out in this country, the "competency rule" is still very much in force almost everywhere except Utah. Our system of law, Irving Prager observes, is based on the assumption that only the jurors decide the facts. "Convicted perjurers can testify. Charles Manson can testify. Adolf Hitler if he were alive today would be allowed to testify. And it would be up to the jury whether to believe these people." Everybody, it seems, can testify, except children. The so-called age of competency varies from state to state but is usually around ten. A child younger than that must first be cross-examined in a separate hearing by the defense attorney and also the judge. Prager still remembers one judge turning to a child and saying, "What is truth? Define truth."

In Utah, which has some of the toughest child-protection laws, the competency rule has been done away with. As in California there's also a mandated prison term for convicted offenders. But strong lobbies were successful in getting through a major exception in the so-called incest-offender category. In many cases this does not mean a blood relative of the abused child, but just someone who lives under the same roof. The mental-health community opines that incestuous fathers frequently have a better prognosis than other types of child molesters. William Prendergast thinks incest can be treated successfully in the home itself, perhaps by putting someone in there—the maternal or paternal grandmother, for example—to stay in the room with the child victim as protection and reassurance for the duration of the father's therapy.

Besides, he says, "I don't see punishing the wife and the children of that family by locking up the breadwinner, having them lose their home, change schools, change their whole socioeconomic base because he has a problem."

He's talking about pure incest situations, not the pedophile who molests his own children along with any others he can get his hands on. Those are much harder cases and may require stronger measures. Maybe a stay at the treatment center.

Not surprisingly, Prager is not impressed with the mental-health community's approach. "There are three things that can happen. One is to put the molester back in the family to molest again, while promising to go to Parents United meetings or whatever. . . . An alternative is to take the child out of the family and leave Daddy there to do whatever he does. So the child goes to a foster home. *She* does the time, in a way. The third possibility, which is almost never done, is to treat the offender as a criminal and put him in prison. It so happens he *is* a criminal."

And so the controversy goes on. The medical men, like Prendergast, want to treat the offender psychologically, cure him by correcting his negative self-image, helping him, in effect, grow up. "When they're with a child," he says, "they feel and behave like a child." They have to learn how to live and function as an adult.

As one convalescing deviate analyzed himself in a recent interview for this book, "Molesters are people who are totally inadequate. . . . They may have preferences as far as adults, but they can't express them the way they want to, so they go to children. But we can't say, 'Well, I just prefer children.' We're doing it because we're copping out. Because we're afraid of normal relationships."

That is certainly a ringing endorsement of the psychotherapeutic approach to the problem. But is it true? Has this man merely convinced himself of this or does he believe it? And to what extent can society feel safe from his possible relapse at some point down the road?

Legislative activists like Irving Prager don't want fellows like this let out into the community to see whether or not they harm more children. Not that Prager is a great believer in prisons. They are certainly unhealthy psychological environments for anybody. Ideally, he says, "we would have a separate area where we could send them so they wouldn't be among children."

"Quarantine" is the word that he thinks applies. "Or a pedophile reservation." He laughs. "Give 'em northern New Jersey, that's my suggestion."

That's easy for *him* to say. He lives in California.

# 20

# *What You Can Do as a Citizen*

As parents our immediate concern is to protect our own children. But then we look down the block and see other children who may also be in danger, children who wander about unsupervised, who haven't been taught the basic safety techniques, and we realize that child protection is not just a family problem—it's a societal problem. And we can help.

We can keep a close eye on the workings of the local day-care center, communicating with other parents and getting together with them to discuss common problems at the center.

For school-age kids we can talk with the principal and the PTA about instituting effective and continuing safety programs in the classrooms.

We can form, or join, local block associations to make sure our immediate neighborhood is properly patrolled and protected. This can involve encouraging the police to be more in evidence, and it can mean forming "citizens' watch" committees. These would *not* be vigilante groups. In fact, they should be formed with the cooperation of the local police. We're talking about a citizen adjunct to the police, not a competing organization. Certainly the police do not need more guns out there in an already jittery community. What they need are more eyes and ears.

Another useful community effort would be the establishment of certain "safe houses" for kids. Preselected neighborhood houses, soda shops, or stores would be designated as safe havens which a child can run into if he feels he's being followed (whether by a molester or by some older kid who wants to take his milk money). One might have special stickers or signs made up and affixed to the entrances of these places.

Some communities agree upon a recognizable distress signal. It may be a certain kind of *yell* that children learn to do when they are in danger. It would be a very different sort of yell from the ordinary screams and hoots of the school yard. Anyone in the community who hears it would come running, yelling the same yell as he goes. It's enough to scare the pants off any molester, or perhaps scare his pants back on. It can have the impact of an Indian war whoop. Some towns may prefer a "whistle alert." All the kids would be provided with the same special kind of whistle, which they'd keep on them at all times and never blow except in emergencies. A child who feels threatened would let out a shrill blast, and all other kids within earshot would blow their own whistles to show that help is on the way.

"Latchkey" kids (as we discussed at the end of Chapter 11) can be better protected if communities institute afterschool programs in the local YMCA, library, or school. Neighboring houses could organize a rotating system of child-minding during the work week. If Jimmy's mom is home on Wednesdays maybe a half-dozen neighborhood latchkeyers could spend Wednesday afternoons over at Jimmy's house. If you have Mondays off maybe you could supervise the gang on Mondays. Get a town meeting convened to work out arrangements so that everybody contributes what he can to the safety of the whole community. A little coordination of effort can give every parent more time for the work he or she has to do. It will also increase the children's safety and decrease parental worries.

As communities band together to protect their children there is an added benefit: a *sense* of community. It's something that's been lost in many parts of our country as people have become more mobile, changed jobs frequently, and lost daily touch with their extended families. But it can be regained, and a community-wide concern for the safety of children can help make it happen. As your neighborhood becomes more cohesive, you may even decide to hold regular town meetings to which kids would be invited and where they could hash over their own safety concerns as well as other matters that affect them. And you don't need a tiny, picturesque New England town, population circa 340, for this to happen. Even the largest American cities are composed of distinct neighborhoods, often with their own character and sets of concerns. Find your neighborhood, join it, and turn it into a communal support system.

Once you know where you stand, and with whom, it is also important to think on wider levels as well—the city and the state. One big problem, which tends to transcend neighborhood boundaries, is with judges who don't seem to view molestation as the deadly serious offense it is. The Adam Walsh Child Resource Center, in Fort Lauderdale, Florida, monitors the court system and periodically gives out embarrassing "Cracked Gavel Awards" to judges who are particularly lax. One Florida judge, Robert Abel, recently received this dubious award after dismissing charges against a man accused of forcing a boy to have sex with him. Abel ruled that the child was not capable of telling the difference between right and wrong and therefore could not testify against his alleged attacker.

And some judges have been on the bench so many years that they've become senile. Dr. Ken Lewis, of Child Custody

Evaluation Services, recently had to deal with an elderly Philadelphia judge who, he says, "took off his robe, threw it on the floor, stomped on it, stood behind the podium, told the stenographer to turn her machine off, raised his arms, and blessed everybody for being alive because *he* was going to go into the back room and *die*." He came out a few minutes later sipping a cup of coffee and, according to Lewis, said, "I didn't die, ha-ha-ha-ha-ha. Now we're going to finish this trial."

The judicial system in this country is deeply entrenched in unexamined tradition and is deeply resistant to change. It should be scrutinized carefully and the bad apples exposed to public criticism. You might want to join, or to form, a judicial-watch committee in your town.

## The Model Legislative Packet

One of the most hopeful developments in the past year is the "model legislative packet" worked out by the Justice Department and the National Center for Missing and Exploited Children. It is a configuration of strong legislative proposals which each state could pass, either in part or as a whole. Parents may want to work for the adoption of such laws in their home state. To get started:

• Find out who your state legislators are.

• Write and/or call them, urging passage of the legislation. Contact representatives from both sides of the legislature if you live in a state with a two-part legislature. Also, contact both Republicans and Democrats. Bipartisan support is essential if such bills are to have a chance of passing.

• Join with organizations that might lobby for these laws. Active organizations include the PTA, local chapters of the League of Women Voters, the Jaycees, the Council of Jewish Women, the Junior League, and the National Education

Association, among others. It's likely that they're lobbying for certain laws already, but perhaps in a hodgepodge way. Find out which of the laws in the "legislative packet" are *not* on the books in your state and—if you believe in their importance—urge the lobbying group of your choice to go for the complete set.

What follows is just a brief summary of some salient points in the packet, published under the title *Selected State Legislation: A Guide for Effective State Laws to Protect Children* (Washington, D.C., National Center for Missing and Exploited Children, 1985). To get this publication write to the center at 1835 K Street, N.W., Suite 700, Washington, D.C. 20006.

### I. Laws on Missing Children

1. There should be a state-level information clearinghouse to collect and disseminate data on missing children in that state as well as to help develop community prevention programs.

2. Also useful is a centralized state-level file on unidentified deceased persons. This would provide backup for the FBI's national (NCIC) computer bank and would require state officials to tie into the NCIC.

3. Eliminate waiting periods before police begin to investigate missing children cases. Now there are often delays of from twenty-four to seventy-two hours.

4. Require the police, after a preliminary investigation, immediately to enter information about missing children into the NCIC computer *and* to notify the FBI promptly when cases entered in the computer have been solved.

### II. Laws on Sexual Abuse and Exploitation

1. Define broadly who must report sexual abuse. Delaware, for instance, legally requires physicians, school employees, social workers, psychologists, medical examiners,

"and any other person" to report cases of child sexual abuse. That means everybody.

2. State laws ought to include sexual abuse and exploitation in their definition of "child abuse." Thus, for instance, child pornography would constitute child abuse, even if the child was not physically harmed or even touched.

3. Some states require that the report be made to a law-enforcement agency or a social service agency. In Florida child abuse by school employees must be immediately reported to the school board.

4. Law-enforcement agencies and social service agencies often don't share information. A law may need to be passed to help them work together.

5. A state law may be needed to ensure temporary protection for an endangered child. In a few states a doctor or police officer can keep a child in his custody for a few days without consent of the parent.

6. Some people don't report child abuse because they're afraid they'll get in legal trouble if they do. Your state may want to legislate immunity for people who report such cases.

7. Your state may also want to legislate penalties for people who *don't* report.

8. Some states have "child protection teams"—seasoned professionals from different disciplines—to handle complicated child-abuse cases.

9. Costly medical examination of sexual abuse victims is usually paid for by the victims' families. It might better be paid out of public funds.

10. Juvenile courts should be legally allowed to issue restraining orders in emergencies to prevent the imminent assault on a child.

11. Limits should be put on the numbers of interviews a child victim should have to endure from social-services folks, the police, therapists, and others.

### III. Criminal Code Provisions

1. The statute of limitations on prosecuting child-abuse cases should be greatly extended—perhaps to fifteen years. Many kids are afraid to report sexual abuse for many years.

2. Some states require proof that a child did not consent to the alleged sex act and others look into the child's prior sexual experiences. Such provisions should be struck down. Many people feel that, certainly below the age of fourteen, the question of consent is inapplicable.

3. Some states have mandatory prison sentences for certain sexual crimes against kids. The drafters of this legislative packet, however, note that this may not work in some incest cases. A child may be reluctant to report the crime—or her family may pressure her to recant—if prison is a mandatory result of conviction. Judges should have some discretion if it's in the *victim's* best interest that the defendant not go to prison.

4. Some states, like Utah and Ohio, mandate the registering of sex offenders with state officials. Utah also requires that the victim be notified before the offender is released.

5. Parole is a big problem. In the case of molesters Utah requires, among other things, that the local prosecutor and the victim(s) be notified of parole hearings and that, once paroled, the parolee undergo three years of outpatient treatment.

### IV. Laws on Courtroom Procedures

1. Some states have thrown out the "competency" rules requiring a child to show that he knows truth from falsehood and can accurately describe details of the abuse. Let the child testify, and let the jury decide whether or not to believe him.

2. Some states now allow the use of leading questions (questions requiring a simple "Yes" or "No") in cases when young kids have trouble articulating detailed sentences. It's one of the more controversial legal innovations.

3. A few states are ruling that out-of-court statements by

children are admissible if the judge thinks the child would be traumatized by testifying in court.

4. Videotaping the child's testimony is allowed in some states, to lessen the child's ordeal, if opportunity for cross-examination is given.

5. Closed-circuit television is another alternative being considered to insulate a terrified child from his or her abuser. All three of these last provisions raise constitutional questions that may ultimately be decided by the Supreme Court.

6. Almost all states have now eliminated the old "corroboration" rules, which stated, in effect, that a child's testimony, by itself, is not good enough to justify a conviction. Other evidence is required. (Such additional evidence seldom exists.)

7. Anatomically correct dolls are permitted in some courts to assist a child victim in testifying. It seems a good idea.

8. Sexual abuse cases can sometimes drag out for a year or more, further traumatizing the victim. Pennsylvania has passed a law requiring prompt disposition of such cases.

9. Several states have adopted a child victim's "bill of rights," urging additional consideration for child witnesses, restraint by the media, help in coping with emotional traumas, simple explanations of legal procedures, and so on.

*V. Laws to Protect the Child's Privacy*
1. Several states keep the name of the child victim confidential in the court records and other documents.

2. Some states rule it a misdemeanor for the news media to publish the name of a sexual assault victim.

3. Those writing this packet feel that even stronger protections are needed.

*VI. Laws for Education and Prevention*
1. A California law requires funding for safety training for schoolchildren "four times in their school career."

2. Laws might also usefully provide for workshops for parents, teachers, and children.

3. Laws might also mandate that new students show records from previous schools or else birth certificates. A kidnapped and relocated child might not have these things.

4. A few states require that lists of missing children within the state be circulated to all schools. These lists would be compared with the student rolls.

### VII.  Background Checks

1. More and more states are requiring criminal history checks for prospective employees in jobs that involve contact with children. This means going through both the state and the federal law-enforcement information systems.

2. Besides checking backgrounds for day-care workers, juvenile-detention employees, and so on, one might legislate criminal conviction checks for foster or adoptive parents.

3. A few states require criminal history checks for anyone involved in the school system. Nobody who's been convicted of a sex offense may be employed in the system.

4. In several states, licenses for child-care institutions will be denied if any of those who operate such facilities have child-abuse or sex-offense convictions.

### VIII.  Training the Professionals

1. Few states mandate sufficient training for law-enforcement and social-service professionals in the critical area of child victimization. They need to be taught effective techniques for dealing with the child victim's needs, interviewing the child, and investigating sex-abuse cases.

2. In-service training programs should also be mandated for prosecutors and judges.

3. Colorado has set up a teacher training program designed to help teachers recognize child-abuse and neglect cases and report them to the right people.

## IX. Treating the Child Victim

1. Social-service agencies should automatically provide treatment and counseling for the child victim. In most states this is not the case, and the victim gets no help at all.

2. Colorado and South Dakota have laws allowing a judge to require the defendant to pay for the rehabilitation and counseling of the child victim.

## X. Court-appointed Advocates

Abandoned, neglected, or abused children are often provided with a special advocate (guardian *ad litem*) to represent their interests and protect their rights. This is not usually true, though, for kids who are simply victims of a crime (e.g., sexual assault). The writers of the packet suggest that the services of a special advocate—independent of the prosecutor and the parents' attorney—be available to any child who is the victim of a crime.

## XI. Parental Kidnapping

1. Many states don't consider child-snatching by a non-custodial parent a felony unless the child is taken out of state. But that's often hard to prove. State laws might be strengthened to make it a felony to steal the child in the first place, and also to conceal the child.

2. States might want to consider making the crime apply also to any individual who assists in the kidnapping.

3. Before custody has been awarded, both parents have custody. But that doesn't mean either parent can take the child and hide him from the other parent. In California you can do a year in jail for trying that. State laws should make penalties clear.

4. California also provides that the absconding parent pay all the expenses incurred in getting the child back.

5. States should work out an arrangement with the Federal Parent Locator Service (established by the Social Secu-

rity Act) to help find missing parents and parentally abducted children.

### XII.  Child Pornography

In 1982 the U.S. Supreme Court (New York v. Ferber) ruled that states could regulate material that shows children involved in sexual activity, even if the material is not legally obscene. This has paved the way for effective state laws. The authors of the packet suggest that such laws accomplish the following:

1. Cover the production, distribution, financing, and reproduction of pornography, plus live shows and pornographic modeling;

2. Specify criminal penalties, even if the material isn't legally obscene;

3. Specify penalties even if there's no profit motive behind the pornography;

4. Apply to all children through their eighteenth birthday;

5. Provide for expert testimony to determine the age of the child portrayed in the pornography;

6. Include penalties for parents or guardians who knowingly let their children be used in pornography.

### XIII.  Child Prostitution

State laws on this subject should accomplish the following:

1. Establish a separate, more serious offense (beyond promoting prostitution generally) for assisting or promoting the prostitution of children;

2. Specify penalties for parents or guardians who knowingly permit children in their care to engage in prostitution;

3. Define "child" as anyone under eighteen;

4. Strike out any statutory language on the books requiring that children involved in prostitution be of "previously chaste behavior";

5. Make it a criminal offense to use the services of a child prostitute—and make it a more serious offense the younger the child is.

If all these proposed laws were on the books in the fifty states, and if they were vigorously enforced by the courts, our children would no doubt be safer than they now are. Not absolutely safe, by any means. There's nothing in this packet to prevent a sick or sadistic person from laying his hands on children. But the kids would have a better chance to escape harm and a better shake in the courts when something does happen. It's a complicated matter, though, trying to legislate for child safety, and reasonable people may disagree about which laws are most useful. Some divorcing parents, for instance, could object to the proposed strictures in the Parental Kidnapping section. When human beings are involved, and passions aroused, it's unlikely that *any* law will seem fair in every case. That's why a judge's discretionary powers are important. A good judge can shape the law to the individual situation. (Of course, that presumes one can always find a good judge.)

# 21

# A Letter Home

Dear Jesse,

We're living in different cities now, and in some ways it seems like different worlds. Now that you're a teenager and increasingly involved with your own friends and concerns, I sometimes worry that we could lose that wonderful closeness we've always had. I guess all parents worry about that.

I remember when you were little and I was taking care of you most weekdays (I don't think the term "house-husband" had yet been coined). You seemed to be wandering obliviously through minefields of danger all the time. I'd run after you and save your neck—from careening cabs, from impending waves, from broken glass, from flaring matches, from snarling dogs. The world seemed bent on destroying you, and you kept smiling seraphically back at it.

Then the day came when your parents could no longer deny you the right to walk to school alone. You and I had retraced those ten blocks together hundreds of times, and there was little danger that you'd lose your way. Yet that first day of independence I secretly followed you, dodging behind buildings lest you turn and catch sight of me. How vulnerable you seemed, and how proud, jaunting down Walnut Street toward school, your lunch box creaking at your side. Although I couldn't at that time really imagine that anyone would want to sexually assault a six-year-old, I was worried, even in my ignorance, that somebody might harm you. Some crazy old drunk, perhaps, or some tough teen. Thank God no one did.

But you had to be allowed independence. Despite all the terrible things I learned about while writing this book, I am convinced that the key to a child's safety lies in his increasing self-reliance. Enlightened, informed, empowered self-reliance. Probably, it helped you to take all those aikido classes too. Regardless of what fancy defensive moves you may have learned and later forgotten, the self-defense classes did give you an agility and a physical/psychological "centeredness" which might help you dodge away from an attack. I think that, as a result, you were a cautious kid, but not a fearful one.

And you weren't isolated, either. Isolation—the sense that no one cares—sometimes makes kids vulnerable to the approaches of child molesters. (And they can be charming guys.) Fortunately, ignorant as I was of that danger, I'd usually be waiting with the other parents on the wall by the playground for school to let out, and then we'd play tag with your pals, and on special days we'd go down to the freight tracks to watch the boxcars grumble past. Your childhood was the best time of my life.

After your mother and I divorced, I wasn't able to see as much of you, especially once I took the job in New York; but we've tried our best, you and I, and I think we've kept pretty honest with each other. Thank God, too, that your mom and I had a calm—even kind—divorce, so there was no temptation for one of us to use you as a pawn to hurt the other. Lots of kids get messed up because their parents are acting like children.

So we may have been lucky, although only you can know if you've come through all of this unharmed. It's time to look ahead.

I can't, as you know, watch over you in the ways I could when you were little and I was there with you. Now that you're fourteen you probably feel that you can look after yourself. To a large extent, this is true. You're stronger and more street-savvy. But you're also—like most kids, I think —extremely generous, willing to assume the best about other people, likely to lend a hand if a stranger asks for help. I hope you don't ever lose those qualities, but *please* keep all your mental antennae out there and waving, and at the first "uh-oh" feeling, at the vaguest hunch that things are not as they should be, get away fast. Don't bother to be polite. You are a very polite kid, Jesse, but that worries me as much as it pleases me. I'm afraid you might let yourself be talked into something (like getting into a stranger's car, or God knows what) because you're afraid of hurting his feelings. Don't be. Several people—one of them an FBI agent—have told me that your age group is the *most* at risk, because you're on your own more and tend to be trusting. I remember being tremendously gullible at your age. It goes with the territory, I guess.

The truth is, I can't save you anymore. I can write a book and make you promise to read it, but the older you get, the more your safety becomes your own responsibility. Then, in surprisingly few years, you may find yourself with a wife and children of your own. Knowing your concern for other people, my guess is that you'll have your heart in your mouth every time they cross the street.

Meanwhile, try to put up with me. I worry about you a lot. And love you a lot.

Stay safe.
Dad

# Appendix:
## Useful Organizations

*NOTE: Inclusion of organizations here does not imply an endorsement of them. Parents must reach their own conclusions.*

ABDUCTED CHILDREN INFORMATION CENTER
*(Computerized registry of missing children)*
1470 Gene Street, Winter Park, FL 32789
305-831-2000

ADAM WALSH CHILD RESOURCE CENTER, INC.
*(Useful information and referrals)*
1876 N. University Drive, Fort Lauderdale, FL 33322
305-475-4847

BAY AREA CENTER FOR VICTIMS OF CHILD STEALING
1165 Meridian Ave., Ste. 112, San Jose, CA 95125
707-544-6536 or 408-425-5134

BERGEN COUNTY MISSING PERSONS BUREAU
*(Data bank on unidentified dead, etc.)*
1 Court Street, Hackensack, NJ 07601
201-646-2192

CENTER FOR EARLY ADOLESCENCE
*(Publications on latchkey and other problems)*
Suite 233, Carr Mill Mall, Carrboro, NC 27510
919-966-1148

CENTER FOR THE FAMILY IN TRANSITION
*(Parental Abductions)*
5725 Paradise Dr., Bldg. A, Suite 100, Corte Madera,
CA 94925
415-924-5750

CHILD ASSAULT PREVENTION PROJECT (CAP)
*(Safety training programs for schools)*
P.O. Box 02084, Columbus, OH 43202
614-291-9751

CHILD FIND
*(Registers missing children; good relationship with media)*
P.O. Box 277, New Paltz, NY 12561
1-800-431-5005
If calling from New York: 914-255-1848

CHILD INDUSTRIES
*(Offers PAT [Prevention Awareness Techniques] Family
Program)*
P.O. Box 26814, Salt Lake City, UT 84126
801-298-2902

CHILD PROTECTION CENTER—SPECIAL UNIT
*(Crisis intervention, treatment, counseling)*
Children's Hospital National Medical Center
111 Michigan Avenue, N.W., Washington, D.C. 20010
202-745-4100

CHILDREN'S RIGHTS OF FLORIDA
*(Helps find missing and abducted children)*
2069 Indian Rock Road, Suite B, Largo, FL 33540
813-584-0888

CHILDREN'S RIGHTS OF NEW YORK, INC.
19 Maple Street, Stony Brook, NY 11790
516-751-7840

CHILD SEARCH
6 Beacon Street, Suite 600, Boston, MA 02108
617-720-1760

CHILD WATCH—USA
P.O. Box 17211, 3815 Interstate Court Suite 201,
Montgomery, AL 36117
205-271-5200

COBRA CONNECTION
*(Publishes* Save a Child *manual, etc.)*
P.O. Box 1958, Station A, Canton, OH 44705-0958
216-454-9109

COVENANT HOUSE—UNDER 21
*(Shelter and counseling for runaways)*
460 West 41st Street, New York, NY 10036
212-613-0300

ECHO (EXPLOITED CHILDREN'S HELP ORGANIZATION)
*(Information center)*
1204 S. 3rd Street, Suite B, Louisville, KY 40203
502-637-8761

FIND-ME, INC.
*(Information center; publishes* Action *booklet)*
P.O. Box 1612, LaGrange, GA 30241-1612
404-884-7419

HEART (HELP EVERY ABDUCTION RETURN TODAY)
*(Parental abductions)*
10937 Red Arrow Highway, Rte. 1, Mattawan, MI 49071
616-668-3733

HIDE AND SEEK FOUNDATION, INC.
*(Investigates cases)*
P.O. Box 806, McMinnville, OR 97218
Branches in Arkansas, Pennslyvania, New Jersey and
California
503-662-3620 or 503-472-3717

MISSING CHILDREN HELP CENTER
*(Referrals)*
410 Ware Boulevard, Suite 1102, Tampa, FL 33619
813-681-HELP or 813-623-KIDS

MISSING CHILDREN NETWORK, THE
*(Syndicated TV show, issues help book, 24-hour hot line)*
Prijatel Productions, Inc.
2211 South Dixie Drive, Dayton OH 45409
1-800-235-3535

MISSING CHILDREN OF AMERICA, INC.
P.O. Box 10-1938, Anchorage, AK 99510
907-243-8484

MISSING PERSONS NATIONWIDE, INC.
P.O. Box 5331, Hudson FL 33568
813-856-5144

MISSING TEENS AND YOUNG ADULTS
*(Sponsors Family Reunion Month)*
P.O. Box 7800, Santa Cruz, CA 95061
408-425-3663 or 408-426-7972

NATIONAL CENTER FOR MISSING AND EXPLOITED CHILDREN
*(Information clearinghouse, referrals, etc.)*
1835 K Street, N.W., Suite 700, Washington, D.C. 20006
hotline: 1-800-843-5678; in Washington, D.C.: 202-634-9836

NATIONAL CHILD SEARCH, INC.
P.O. Box 800038, Oklahoma City, OK 73180
405-685-5621

NATIONAL COALITION FOR CHILDREN'S JUSTICE
2998 Shelburne Road, Shelburne, VT 05482
802-985-8458

NATIONAL COUNCIL ON CHILD ABUSE AND FAMILY VIOLENCE
1050 Connecticut Ave., N.W., Washington, D.C. 20036
202-429-6695

NATIONAL CRIME PREVENTION COUNCIL
*(Information and action kits for schools and parents)*
1341 G. Street, N.W., Suite 706, Washington, D.C. 20005
202-393-7141

NATIONAL "KID PRINT" PROGRAM
*(Child fingerprinting information)*
P.O. Box 5548, Buena Park, CA 90622
714-983-0945

NATIONAL MISSING CHILDREN'S LOCATE CENTER, INC.
*(Publishes* Children's Action Network Directory*)*
P.O. Box 42584, Portland, OR 97242
503-238-1350

NATIONAL RUNAWAY SWITCHBOARD
*(24 hours, counseling, message relays, confidential)*
2210 North Halstead, Chicago, IL 60614
1-800-621-4000
Illinois only: 1-800-972-6004

NATION WIDE MISSING PERSONS BUREAU
3500 Aldine Bender, Box A, Houston, TX 77032
713-449-0355 or 713-449-3449

OKLAHOMA PARENTS AGAINST CHILD STEALING
*(Assists in recovery of children)*
P.O. Box 2112, Barlesville, OK 74005
918-534-1489

OPERATION PEACE OF MIND
*(24 hours, counseling, message relays, confidential)*
P.O. Box 52896, Houston, TX 77052
1-800-231-6946
Texas only: 1-800-392-3352

PARENTS ANONYMOUS
*(Self-help groups to stop physical abuse)*
Various chapters in U.S.
1-800-421-0358
New York only: 1-800-462-6406

PARENTS OF MURDERED CHILDREN
*(Outreach and support)*
1739 Bella Vista, Cincinnati, OH 45237
513-721-LOVE or 513-242-8025

PARENTS UNITED
   *(Incest therapy and counseling)*
   Various chapters in U.S., based in San Jose, CA
   408-280-5055

PARENTS WITHOUT PARTNERS
   *(Concerns of single parents and their children)*
   Various chapters in U.S.
   7910 Woodmont Avenue, Suite 1000, Bethesda, MD 20814
   1-800-638-8078

PHONE FRIEND, INC.
   *(Offers information to set up "warm lines" for latchkey kids)*
   American Association of University Women
   P.O. Box 735, State College, PA 16804
   814-234-3355

SAFE (THE SAFETY AND FITNESS EXCHANGE)
   *(Safety programs for schools, plus martial arts training for kids)*
   541 Avenue of the Americas, New York, NY 10011
   212-242-4874

SEXUAL ASSAULT CENTER, THE
   *(Crisis intervention, treatment, counseling)*
   Harborview Medical Center, Seattle, WA
   206-223-3000

SLAM (SOCIETY'S LEAGUE AGAINST MOLESTATION)
   *(Lobbies for strong legislation, offers "Cautious Kid" programs)*
   Various chapters in U.S.
   303-755-5800

VOCAL (VICTIMS OF CHILD ABUSE LAWS)
   *(Helps parents unjustly accused of molesting children)*
   5571 210th Street East, Hampton, MN 55031
   612-871-0348

# Bibliography

Armstrong, Louise. *Kiss Daddy Goodnight*. New York: Hawthorn Books, 1978.

*Attorney General's Task Force on Family Violence—Final Report*. U.S. Department of Justice, Sept., 1984.

Bach, G. R., and P. Wyden. *The Intimate Enemy*. New York: Avon Books, 1968.

Baker, Nancy C. *Babyselling: The Scandal of Black Market Adoptions*. New York: Vanguard, 1978.

Bell, Alan P. *The Personality of the Child Molester*. Chicago: Aldine, Atherton, 1971.

Brady, Katherine. *Father's Days*. New York: Seaview, 1979.

Clinkscales, John Dixon. *Kyle's Story: Friday Never Came*. New York: Vantage, 1981.

Colao, Flora, and Tamar Hosansky. *Your Children Should Know*. Indianapolis and New York: Bobbs-Merrill, 1983.

Densen-Gerber, Dr. Judianne. *Physical and Sexual Abuse of Children*. New York: Odyssey Institute, Inc., 1981.

Finkelhor, D. *Sexually Victimized Children*. New York: Free Press, 1979.

Fontana, Dr. Vincent J. *Somewhere a Child is Crying: Maltreatment—Causes and Prevention*. New York: Macmillan, 1973.

Gelles, Richard J. *The Violent Home*. Beverly Hills: Sage Publications, 1974.

Gil, D. G. *Violence Against Children: Physical Child Abuse in the United States*. Cambridge: Harvard University Press, 1970.

Gordon, Dr. Thomas. *P.E.T.—Parent Effectiveness Training.* New York: Peter H. Wyden, Inc., 1970. (New American Library, 1975.)

Hackshaw, Dr. Eugenia, Dr. James O. F. Hackshaw, and Stephen F. Hutchinson. *A Conceptual Model for the Study of Some Abusing Parents: A Sociological Autopsy.* New York: Odyssey Institute, Inc., 1979.

Hechinger, Grace. *How to Raise a Street-Smart Child.* New York: Facts on File, 1984.

Herbruck, Christine C. *Breaking the Cycle of Child Abuse.* Minneapolis: Winston Press, 1979.

Kelly, J. A. *Treating Child Abusive Families—Intervention Based on Skills-Training Principles.* New York: Plenum, 1984.

Kempe, C. H., and R. E. Helfer, eds. *Helping the Battered Child and his Family.* Philadelphia: Lippincott, 1974.

*Kids Go to Court, Too.* Booklet from Hennepin County Attorney's Office, Sexual Assault Services, C-2100 Government Center, Minneapolis, MN 55487.

Kroth, Jerome A. *Child Sexual Abuse.* Springfield, IL: Thomas, 1979.

Lanning, Kenneth, and Ann Wolbert Burgess. "Child Pornography and Sex Rings." FBI Law Enforcement Bulletin (January 1984), pp. 10–16.

Lefstein, Leah M., William Kerewsky, Elliott A. Medrich, and Carol Frank. *3:00 to 6:00 P.M.: Young Adolescents at Home and in the Community.* Carrboro, NC: Center for Early Adolescence, 1982.

Marsano, William. *The Street-Smart Book.* New York: Wanderer, 1985.

Meyer, Linda D. *Safety Zone.* Washington: The Charles Franklin Press, 1984.

O'Brien, Shirley. *Child Abuse, A Crying Shame.* Provo, UT: Brigham Young University Press, 1980.

———. *Child Pornography.* Dubuque, IA: Kendall-Hunt, 1983.

Prager, Irving. " 'Sexual Psychopathy' and Child Molesters: The Experiment Fails." *Journal of Juvenile Law,* Vol. 6 (1982), pp. 49–79.

Rush, Florence. *The Best Kept Secret—Sexual Abuse of Children.* New York: McGraw-Hill, 1980.

Sanford, Linda T. *The Silent Children.* New York: Doubleday, 1980.

———. *Come Tell Me Right Away: A Positive Approach to Warning Children About Sexual Abuse.* Fayetteville, NY: Ed-U Press, 1982.

*Selected State Legislation: A Guide for Effective State Laws to Protect Children.* Washington, D.C.: National Center for Missing and Exploited Children, 1985.

Strauss, Murray A., Richard J. Gelles, and Suzanne K. Steinmetz. *Behind Closed Doors: Violence in the American Family.* New York: Doubleday, 1980.

Wachter, Oralee. *No More Secrets For Me.* Boston: Little, Brown, 1983.

Walters, David R. *Physical and Sexual Abuse of Children: Causes and Treatment.* Bloomington, IN: Indiana University Press, 1975.

Wein, Bibi. *The Runaway Generation.* New York: McKay, 1970.

Wooden, Ken. *Child Lures: A Guide to Prevent Abduction.* Mascoutah, IL: Ralston Purina Company, 1984. (Also available from ABC-TV News.)

# *Index*